JACKIE LEAC

PLAYING IN TH

GENETICS, ETHICS AN

SWARTHMORE LECTURE 2002
QUAKER *Q* BOOKS

First published in May 2002 by Quaker Books
Friends House, Euston Road, London NW1 2BJ

http://www.quaker.org.uk

ISBN 0 85245 337 X

Design & typesetting: Jonathan Sargent
Printed by Thanet Press Ltd
Text typeface: ITC Charter 10.5 on 15pt

We thank Bridgeman Picture Library for permission to show details from the ceiling of the Sistine Chapel, Vatican City, painted by Michelangelo Buonarroti in 1510. The copyright holders have kindly given permission to use excerpts from works on the following pages: on page 1, 'Curiosity', *Weathering* by Alastair Reid courtesy of the author; p.7 'Vacillation', courtesy of Scribner, a division of Simon & Schuster Inc. from *The Collected Works of WB Yeats: Volume I, The Poems*, Revised Edition, ed. Richard J Finneran © 1933 The Macmillan Company, © renewed 1961 Bertha Georgie Yeats; p.25 'All for science', *archyology* by Don Marquis courtesy of Bloodaxe Books; p.66 'Touch', *Selected Poems 1950–1975* by Thom Gunn courtesy of Faber & Faber; p.84 'The Waking' © 1952 Theodore Roethke from *The Collected Poems of Theodore Roethke* by Theodore Roethke courtesy of Doubleday, a division of Random House Inc and in the UK, Faber & Faber; p.100 'Love is a Parallax', *Collected poems* by Sylvia Plath courtesy of Faber & Faber (except in USA) and in USA courtesy of Harper Collins Publishers.

PREFACE

The Swarthmore Lectureship was established by the Woodbrooke Extension Committee at a meeting held December 9, 1907: the minute of the Committee providing for an 'annual lecture on some subject relating to the message and work of the Society of Friends'. The name Swarthmore was chosen in memory of the home of Margaret Fox, which was always open to the earnest seeker after Truth, and from which loving words of sympathy and substantial material help were sent to fellow workers.

The lectureship has a twofold purpose: first, to interpret to the members of the Society of Friends their message and mission; and secondly, to bring before the public the spirit, the aims and fundamental principles of Friends. The lecturers alone are responsible for any opinions expressed.

The lectureship provides both for the publication of a book and for the delivery of a lecture, the latter usually at the time of assembly of Britain Yearly Meeting of the Society of Friends. A lecture related to the present book was delivered at Yearly Meeting in London on the evening of May 4, 2002.

DEDICATION

Debby Plummer was the first person to embody for me the truth that science and religion shine different lights on the whole, and so this book is for her.

CONTENTS

Acknowledgements   IX

Terminology   XI

1   A view over the territory   1

2   Genetics in the twentieth century, and after   13

3   Ethical issues in gene technology   25

4   At play in the fields of the Lord   48

5   Ethics in relationship   66

6   A Quaker approach   84

Glossary   104

Bibliography   108

Taking it further:

Reading   109

Getting involved and informed   112

Study questions   114

ACKNOWLEDGEMENTS

First of all, I want to record my deep gratitude to the Swarthmore Lecture Committee for giving me the excuse to think harder about difficult questions. Working on this book has transformed my thinking in many ways, and I can't imagine being given a better gift.

Ideas that found their way into the book were sparked, nourished, challenged, torn to pieces and sent off in new directions by many different people. I have relied, probably more than they realised, on Richard Harper, Jennifer Jenkins, Alison Peacock, Debby Plummer (who pointed me in the direction of Proverbs), Christoph Rehmann-Sutter, Michael Royston, Chris Skidmore and Markus Zimmermann-Acklin. Tracey Dixon gave up part of her Christmas holiday to test-run the Glossary. I hope they can spot how much their comments and criticisms have improved the book, and that they forgive me for all the stimulating suggestions that I couldn't incorporate because they would have tripled its length.

I particularly want to thank the members of the Grundlagen group of the Swiss Society for Biomedical Ethics, and the Feminist Approaches to Bioethics Network, for the nicest possible intolerance of waffly thought. I have been much helped by conversations with Amber Carroll, Joy Bell and others of the Quaker Genetics and Ethics Network. Pam Lunn and John Lampen, on the Swarthmore Lecture Committee, were enthusiastic and encouraging and asked the sort of questions that improve without demoralising. I also thank the other members of the Committee for their thought-ful and experienced input, and Janet Scott, Alex Wildwood, Tony Stoller, Tim Newell and Gil Skidmore for diverse forms of support at opportune times.

Margaret Spufford has consistently urged me not to confuse seriousness with solemnity. A birthday Tarot by Luzia Sutter Rehmann was instrumental in making me write what I really thought. Over the years Anna Bidder instructed me in microscopy without eyestrain, welcomed me to Jesus Lane Meeting, and reassured me when I was struggling with the transition from mol-ecular biology to bioethics. I wish she had lived to see this book.

Most of the serious writing was done during several periods at Woodbrooke Quaker Study Centre. Keeping the Swarthmore Lec-turer's identity confidential meant that when people asked what I was working on, my answers were suspiciously evasive; it's a measure of the spirit of Woodbrooke that they were accepted without comment. My thanks are due to everyone there but espe-cially to Jennifer Barraclough, Doug Gwyn, Ben Pink Dandelion, Pam Lunn, Rachel Milling, Marion McNaughton and Leonora Wilson for words in passing, long talks, discretion, and letting me be as unsociable as I liked.

Much of this book had its origins somewhere in my 17-year conversation with Alison Peacock on biology, ethics, spiritual journeys, love, feminism, and the iniquities of organised religion. Monica Buckland Hofstetter remains my most reliable intellectual gadfly and pretentiousness detector. She also taught me about music, and the value of enjoyment.

A NOTE ABOUT TERMINOLOGY

Writing about gene technology inevitably means using some technical jargon, although I have tried to keep this to a minimum. Scientific terms that may be unfamiliar are usually defined on first use, and there is also a glossary at the back of the book.

Some Friends may have difficulty with the theological vocabulary I use. As will become clear, my theology is consistent with a continuing creation and a creator active within and beyond it, and in general I have found conventional theological language to be useful. I'm not a theological purist, however, and I would much rather that Friends feel free to translate terminology they find meaningless into something more acceptable, than that they stop reading.

I

A VIEW OVER THE TERRITORY

Curiosity
will not cause us to die –
only lack of it will.
Never to want to see
the other side of the hill,
or that improbable country
where living is an idyll...
Alastair Reid, Curiosity

Reproductions of Michelangelo's *Creation of Adam* on the ceiling of the Sistine Chapel tend to focus on what the right hand of God is doing. The composition of the painting directs all our attention towards God animating the reclining figure of Adam and away from the little cluster on the other side. The woman being cradled in the crook of God's left arm is easily overlooked, as is often the case with women. Yet this figure is identified as Sophia, the personification of Wisdom. According to the Book of Proverbs she is part of the Creation: 'The Lord created me the beginning of his works, before all else that he made, long ago. Alone, I was fashioned in times long past, at the beginning, long before earth itself.' Michelangelo's Wisdom is watching the creation of humankind with an expression of curiosity, alertness, and half a smile. She doesn't seem to be taking the proceedings with unconditional seriousness, and she looks on the verge of joining in.

This book and the related lecture are about ethical decisions in genetic manipulation. The last half of the twentieth century saw an explosion in our understanding of genetics and molecular biology; the questions now are in what form that genetic understanding will be put to use, and how and by whom it will be controlled. There are already thousands of patents on genes, and dozens of field trials of genetically modified crops underway, and most hospitals, diagnostic services and research institutes could not operate without genetic manipulation in some form. The task is therefore not to decide whether gene technology should happen, because it already has, but to ensure that it is implemented ethically and sustainably, with consideration of the rights of other people present and to come, and of the rest of the natural world.

Since this isn't a detective novel I have no inhibitions about giving away the content of the following chapters and what happens in the end. Chapters 2 and 3 provide an outline of some key areas of gene technology and the associated ethical issues. Chapter 4 discusses ideas about play; it should become clear that this is not a digression, but provides some important clues to thinking about the ethical practice of science. I trace the path taken by my own thinking, including ideas I eventually rejected, as I identified elements important to the art of play. They include the significance of relationships, and chapter 5 explores the meaning of relationship in ethics and in the ethics of genetics. Finally, in chapter 6 I try to draw these ideas together with suggestions for a Quaker approach to ethical gene technology. These suggestions are meant to be a starting point for Britain Yearly Meeting's corporate exploration, and not a blueprint for action.

This first chapter, however, is about science and spirituality, and how the two are connected. It was not my original intention to venture into this area. It seemed important, however, to describe my reasons for becoming a scientist in the first place, and to explain why science is still important to me. In doing so it became impossible not to write about spiritual experience.

I want to consider that the fundamental impulse that drives scientists can be rooted in a spirituality, so that 'doing science' can be another way of 'doing a relationship with God' as much as prayer or meeting for worship, or listening to music, or experiencing nature in a landscape. This is contentious because in the last half-century or so, attitudes towards science and technology have undergone radical change. Once upon a time – it seems ancient history now – there was a fairly universal belief in the ideal of continuing progress, with science providing much of that progress in terms of acknowledged goods like improved living conditions, better healthcare, increased leisure, and so on. Scientific progress was also seen as contributing to the overall improvement of the human condition; material progress would be accompanied by moral and spiritual improvement, leading slowly but inevitably to the establishment of the kingdom of heaven on earth. Widespread scientific optimism ended with the development, and more particularly the use, of nuclear weapons. The years since then have seen an irreversible loss of faith in science's benevolence and ability to make the world a better place (although not necessarily in its ability simply to drive material development).

Gene technology is no exception. The Society of Friends and the wider society have legitimate concerns about the direction gene technology is taking and the purposes for which it will be used. It is important to be clear from the outset that I do not think these concerns are trivial, unfounded or easily resolved. What is worrying, however, is where suspicion about science is eroding any feeling for why it is done in the first place. It may be this is no great loss: few people earn their living as scientists, most aren't particularly interested in it as an endeavour, and all of us are only too aware of its dark side. But I think it *is* a loss. For one thing, historically the Society of Friends has had an unusually fruitful relationship with science and technology. The reasons for this are social and theological, and not entirely clear, but the end result is that there have been eminent Quaker scientists in every century, including the chemists John Dalton and William Allen, physicists and astronomers Arthur Eddington, Thomas Young, Kathleen Lonsdale and Jocelyn Bell Burnell, and physicians Thomas Hodgkin and Joseph Lister. If that link were to become purely nostalgic because science is no longer something we care to be associated with, it would indicate some disturbing things about the Society of Friends today and its distance from the rest of the world.

It would also be a profound religious loss because scientific investigation of all kinds offers paths into creation that – in my experience – run parallel to the ones that mystics take, and tend to end up in the same place. Saying this does not mean I endorse the sort of natural theology that uses bits of scientific data either as evidence for the existence of God, or as hints towards the nature of God – except very obscurely. I would rather talk about curiosity being one of our most human characteristics, and scientific exploration as an expression of curiosity that says something noteworthy about our relationship with God and with creation.

In this chapter I refer mostly to the 'science' half of the 'science and technology' coupling. Very roughly, they can be distinguished by saying science investigates how the universe is, and technology puts that knowledge into practice. In gene technology, the science side is the study of the mechanisms of inheritance and development; the technological side is its implementation as genetic diagnosis, or GM food. The interaction between science and technology is complicated, and there are enough areas of overlap for it to be a continuum rather than a dichotomy. (It is certainly not the sharp dichotomy used by some apologists for science, which goes 'Science good, technology bad'.)

I have said that scientific exploration can be a spiritual path. A claim like this is only convincing if it comes from experience, and so I need to spend some time describing my own. Situating myself may also help to put the rest of the book into context.

In one sense, I'm a scientist because of my educational choices. After the age of 16 the subjects I specialised in were scientific, and I spent four years at university studying biochemistry. In the final year of the course we carried out a small research project under supervision. I enjoyed this very much, partly because it produced a result, a phenomenon that was not often repeated in my research career. I went on to do a PhD, spending four years unravelling how a particular gene was involved in breast cancer. Most of my time was spent in the unglamorous, uninspiring (not to say uninspired) scut work of the graduate student apprenticeship. In the end, I was able to prove convincingly that my favourite gene was remarkably *uninvolved* in breast cancer, a prime illustration of the recalcitrance of nature that is the everyday reality of scientific research.

This is what it says on my CV about my scientific training. What it doesn't say is that I went into science for the religion. These steps in a scientific career are only the outward and visible signs of an inward drive to *understand* that is part of my make-up and that I believe is present in all of us. Some of us respond to it by going on pilgrimages, others by going into labs.

In my childhood and adolescence I had experiences I can only call mystical, despite being not entirely comfortable with using that kind of vocabulary. Each occasion was, for me, a clear opening into the presence of God. These events were almost always allied to a sudden, epiphanic moment of *understanding something* about the natural world. And although in each case my entry point was through thinking scientifically, the trajectory of understanding went much further.

I can date one of these to my first year at secondary school. I had been reading some popular books about cosmology and my head was full of thoughts about black holes, the Big Bang, the expanding universe and so on. A point these books emphasised was the immense age of the universe and how incomprehensible it was. You can grasp the size of a week, a month, or a year; you can 'get it' intellectually and also aesthetically, you can feel it in your bones. 'Getting' the bulk of 15 billion years is a different matter altogether. I had been playing with the idea for a while, enjoying a frisson at the thought of this unimaginably vast stretch of time, when suddenly, without my trying – without my even knowing that I could try – I 'got' it. There was a feeling like the sudden give of an elastic band when you stretch it too far, then time came apart. There was *for ever*, and I disappeared into it.

It's not my purpose to describe what happened, but if I were to try I would have no choice but to use the language of the mystics, who return from their voyages with reports of the unity of all things, of having no boundaries, of losing oneself but still not being afraid. And although my experience was essentially an impersonal insight into cosmic time, it took place, in a way I cannot explain rationally, in the context of a presence. I am not claiming this experience was anything unique; many people have similar moments of insight. The point I want to make is that it was one of the most religious moments of my life, and it was contemplation of a scientific idea that got me there.

Wanting to know the answers to *how* and *why* is a desire for comprehension, which can find expression in science, but runs deeper than just being intrigued by what makes things go. It has to do with the desire for communion – an engagement with 'the other', in this case on an intellectual level, which encloses that other within one's own horizon of understanding. This engagement can occur in a variety of forms, running from scientific investigation to contemplative prayer and back. Once again, I can most clearly illustrate it by a specific example. One afternoon in the summer holidays when I was about 13, I was reading a book about physical chemistry. (It should be only too obvious by now that I was a nerd.) The chapter I was reading gave an account of valency. This theory explains how the atomic structure of different chemical elements like sodium and chlorine, determines the kinds of compounds they can form: some are able to combine (sodium and chlorine give sodium chloride, or salt) and others cannot. The theory explains on an atomic level why some compounds occur and others that you might imagine should exist do not. The explanation made sense to me. It made meaningful a lot of things that had previously appeared totally arbitrary.

This explains why I found reading about valency intellectually satisfying. I remember the excitement very clearly: I rocked backwards and stuck my legs in the air with enjoyment. But it went much further than intellectual satisfaction. When I grasped with my mind what valency was all about, I also had a warm sense of being at home in the universe. Everything, not just my appreciation of chemical compounds, fell into a new alignment that turned its face towards me in a friendly way. It was something to do with realising that understanding was founded on the rightness of my being there to understand: being who I was, where I was, when I was; and on the rightness of the relationship with what I was being given to understand. This broke over me with an intensity I am incapable of describing. The only thing that has ever come close is a stanza by Yeats that I found years later:

> While on the shop and street I gazed
> My body, of a sudden, blazed;
> And twenty minutes more or less,
> It seemed, so great my happiness
> That I was blessed and could bless.

> (WB Yeats, Vacillation)

This event informs my belief that understanding is about communion. I reject the widespread notion that all knowledge is instrumental (that it's good because you can do things like build bridges and cure disease with it), or that knowledge *necessarily* has anything to do with power. The picture of the mad scientist hell-bent on world domination has become a cliché precisely because it conforms to what many people believe. Some ethicists have also taken a darker view of knowledge. The Jewish philosopher

Emmanuel Levinas, for example, argued that 'knowing' always involves distancing and domination. He believed that attempts to know something else ('the Other') could only succeed by reducing the Other to 'the Same'. Knowing something therefore involves the destruction of what is truly different about the Other, as we strong-arm it into our own region of understanding, forcing it to comply with our comprehension of it.

Of course, knowledge can sometimes be like that. But it is not how I experienced knowing in my valency event. I wasn't a particularly good person when I was 13, and if knowledge had then held any invitation to become master of the universe I would have been as keen as anyone – but it didn't. My experience was that as much as I drew *whatever was out there* into my understanding, I was also being pulled into the understanding of *whatever was out there*.

∞

Since the mid-1970s there has been a distinct shift in the relationship between science and religion. Many more people now appear interested in reconciling the two, or say that reconciliation is unnecessary because there is no fundamental incompatibility. Theologians, and some scientists, are now willing to acknowledge that the scientific and religious approaches are complementary rather than antagonistic. It has also become more acceptable to admit to the spiritual impulses within science, and authors of books about physics and cosmology often make excursions into the realm of the mystical or religious. There are books with titles like *God and the New Physics*, or *The Fire in the Equations*; a key example of the genre, Hawking's *A Brief History of Time*, ends with his overheated line, 'if we find the answer to [the question of why we and the universe exist] it would be the ultimate triumph of human reason – for then we would know the mind of God' (Hawking, 1990: 175).

The biological and medical sciences have been comparatively neglected in this rapprochement. This is odd, because these disciplines have been through a growth phase over the past 20 to 30 years, and molecular genetics is now rarely out of the news. The sequencing of genes has become fast and routine, genetically manipulated animals are commonplace in the laboratory, we are starting to piece together the molecular interactions that keep cells going, molecular diagnosis has moved into the clinic; the presentation of the first draft sequence of the entire human genome in June 2000 was a milestone, even if a largely symbolic one. With all this in mind it is strange that although the *ethical* implications of the genetic revolution are widely discussed, not much thought has yet been given to its meaning in religious and spiritual terms.

One reason for this is that biology is messy, and we like our spirituality clean. When I finished Finals, a friend wrote to congratulate me on getting a degree 'in things that go squish in the body', a line which accurately expresses the religious attitude to biological materiality. Christianity is officially an incarnational religion, but it is shaped by its Hellenic roots and a subsequent history that was much more comfortable with the transcendent than the immanent. In practice it has tended to cope with the burden of being incarnational by having as little to do with carnality as possible. There are certainly minority traditions within Christianity – one example is Celtic spirituality – that seek unity with rather than alienation from the natural world, but even then a distancing from the materiality of our *bodies* is sometimes still detectable. This religious history is one of the reasons why it can be easier to get a mystical high from the contemplation of distant stars, or the grandeur of a terrestrial landscape, than from, say, blood clotting.

But I went into science for the religion and I found it in molecular genetics. Most of us have difficulty talking about the deepest levels of motivation for what we do. Scientists, like other people, are motivated by a complex muddle of noble and less noble reasons and, also like other people, they tend to construct out of this muddle a rationale they can live with and can bear admitting to others. At my university entrance interview I said I wanted to study biochemistry because I liked biology and chemistry (and it must have sounded plausible enough to get me in), and because a biochemistry degree offered a reasonable chance of postgraduate employment. The fact that, year after year, I had made a habit of falling in love with my biology teachers, one of whom had read biochemistry at the university I eventually went to, also played a bigger part than I was once able to admit. But by far the hardest reason for me to talk about – and it certainly wasn't one I gave then – is that biochemistry and molecular biology tell me a spiritual story about life as well as a scientific one. Biochemistry is concerned with the chemical reactions that build and maintain organisms. It turns out that the vast majority of the chemical reactions in processes like respiration, digestion, responses to external stimuli and so on, are universal. You do not have to learn a biochemistry of the sea urchin, then a different one for the fruit fly and yet another for the elephant. Because evolutionary processes are essentially conservative, if a metabolic pathway is working adequately in one biological context it's likely to continue being used, with modifications as required, rather than be replaced by something different.

However straightforward the evolutionary reason, I found – and still find – this underground unity stunning. At a genetic level, it is a story about unity unfolding into diversity, and diversity unfolding to reveal, at its heart, unity. Embodied in cells and tissues, in biochemical reactions and molecular processes, are the mystics' reports of universal oneness.

Becoming conscious of this is not a dramatic irruption of awareness like the ones I described earlier, but once taken on board there is no going back. Every moment of every encounter, with all forms of life on this planet, is shot through with this biochemical kinship, a continuing revelation of immanence to counterpart the transcendence that people can find in physics and cosmology. For me, an unavoidable component of this awareness is the demand it makes, and this differentiates it from those experiences with time and valency. Discovering a sense of the numinous in cosmic time or subatomic structure had the impact of a revelation, but it did not require me to be transformed at the mundane level of relationship with other living things or with my own corporeality.

Engagement with contemporary molecular biology is challenging because it demands a response that leaves us other than we were. But while this consciousness may alter our relationships with other beings, or call on us to make some kind of restorative action, it is important to be aware of its limits. It may provide some ethical indicators, but it does not – cannot – tell us directly what to do. As with the scriptures, we can't extract behavioural guidelines straight from the text. That isn't what the text, or the data, are there for. An awareness of mystical unity does not *by itself* indicate whether it is morally permissible to use animals for experiments, or genetically manipulate plants, or perform prenatal genetic diagnosis, or clone human beings.

I will be returning to some of these issues later on. My main focus will be gene technology applied to human beings, because this is the area I know something about. Moreover, it is in the form of genetic medicine that gene technology will touch the lives of most of us in very personal and concrete ways that require us to make choices, or at least have opinions. A final, important reason is that these topics are morally ambiguous. Although the ethics of war or environmentalism are far from straightforward, I think many more people could state that destroying the rainforest is wrong, than could be so unequivocal about prenatal genetic testing leading to abortion, or even about human cloning. Not only do we not yet have enough experience of gene technology to foresee *what* its possible consequences might be, let alone evaluate them morally; we don't yet have a consensus on *how* to interpret the capabilities of gene technology in terms of our moral and social values.

This book is a foray into that territory. Some Friends will be disappointed that I make no attempt to provide solutions to current genetic ethical problems, to say whether cloning or prenatal testing are wrong, or at the very least give a few basic rules for making ethical decisions in gene technology. I don't, because ethics are based on moral evaluations, which are (in part) personal. It's one thing to give my personal opinions, as I do freely in this book, but they are coloured by my background and biases: I don't anticipate that any solutions I could put forward would be generally acceptable to Friends or anyone else. More fundamentally, in a morally contentious area like gene technology whose effects are felt throughout society, there may never be such things as unequivocally right answers. Instead, what we should be on the look out for are approaches, attitudes and compromises that we can agree are aligned with the good, and that most of us can live with.

2

GENETICS IN THE TWENTIETH CENTURY, AND AFTER

We have come a long way on that old molecule.
Lewis Thomas, The Medusa and the Snail

Despite the title, this chapter is not a history of genetics and molecular biology over the last hundred years. I am not an historian, and several excellent and accessible histories are already available (some are suggested at the back of the book). Nor is it an attempt at a comprehensive treatment of contemporary molecular genetics. The rate of change in a technically driven area like gene technology means that any account would be dated within months, and superseded within an embarrassingly few years. What I want to do is provide a background for the rest of the book, by tracing some major developments in molecular genetics and looking at how they changed our ideas about inheritance and the role of molecular processes in development and disease. This background is necessarily superficial; but one message to take from this (which I will return to later on) is that it is not necessary to have a detailed understanding of genetics to develop opinions about its ethical use.

Early days

The words and concepts of genetics – gene, genome, DNA – have become so familiar we tend to forget that up to halfway through the twentieth century the actual material of inheritance, the nature of what is passed on from parent to offspring, was a puzzle. (This absence was a particularly acute embarrassment for evolutionary theory. What did natural selection actually select?) Most geneticists thought the genetic material was probably some kind of protein, because proteins vary enormously in size, shape and other characteristics, and only they seemed diverse enough to account for the diversity of organisms. It was not until 1944 that three Americans, Oswald Avery, Colin MacLeod and Maclyn McCarty, did experiments to show that if one species of bacteria was given DNA from another species, the phenotype (the physical characteristics) of the recipients was permanently changed. This apparently trivial result was a crucial indicator that DNA, the chemical deoxyribonucleic acid, was *in some way* a carrier of genetic information. The '*in some way*' part remained unsolved. How do you go from a molecule which is chemically not very variable, whose structure is so regular it can be crystallised, to the huge variety and irregularity of characteristics transmitted genetically?

The resolution of this puzzle began when the structure of DNA was determined in the early 1950s, through the efforts of Rosalind Franklin, Maurice Wilkins, Francis Crick and James Watson. The two-stranded, twisted architecture of DNA – the double helix – was worked out using the methods of X-ray crystallography, a process roughly equivalent to unravelling a woollen sweater, shining a light through the resulting tangle of wool, and trying to deduce from the shadows on the wall what the original knitting pattern looked like. The surprising thing is that it worked at all. The structure they deduced was not only consistent with the crystallographic data, but aesthetically satisfying as well. As is often the case in biology, structure and function are closely related, and knowing the structure also gave important clues to the mechanisms of the biological processes in which DNA is involved: how DNA does the business of transmitting genetic information.

It is now clear that DNA is a very large molecule, made up of individual chemical subunits called nucleotides or bases, and the sequence of these nucleotides provides the instructions for assembling the proteins that are some of the most important structural and chemical components of living things. Molecular biologists think of 'a gene' as the stretch of DNA coding for a protein, or sometimes a whole set of related proteins. (In other disciplines – for example, evolutionary biology – genes are defined in different ways, and in fact molecular biology itself has more than one definition, as I discuss later in this chapter.) When a particular protein is required, the appropriate sequence of DNA nucleotides is read off (transcribed) into a slightly different molecule called messenger RNA (mRNA). In turn, mRNA is converted or 'translated' into protein by another bit of cellular machinery. What remains largely unexplained is how the time and space-specific expression of genes is controlled – how the body ensures, usually successfully, that out of the tens of thousands of genes in the genome, the right one becomes active at the right time, in the right tissue, and produces the right amount of the required protein.

Gene technology

The history of molecular biology demonstrates that conceptual developments in science tend to go hand in hand with technical ones. First, the techniques of X-ray crystallography were a prerequisite for investigating the three-dimensional structure of DNA. No crystallography, no structure – at least not in 1953. Most of the painstaking unravelling of the mechanism of transcription and translation made use of experiments with bacteria, and was dependent on sophisticated microbiological techniques. And molecular biology was turned into gene technology by the technically important discovery of *restriction enzymes*.

The word 'breakthrough' has been cheapened by the popular media's usage of it as a synonym for 'result', but the discovery of restriction enzymes genuinely broke through a frustrating technical barrier. Restriction enzymes are bacterial proteins, which have evolved as protective devices. Like humans, bacteria can be infected by viruses, and like human viruses these *bacteriophages* hijack the bacterial cell by replacing its genetic instructions with viral genetic information. Bacteria developed restriction enzymes to cut the genetic material of invading viruses into pieces before a takeover can happen.

From the human point of view, the important thing is that these enzymes – several hundred of which have been isolated – cut DNA at very specific sites indicated by a particular short stretch of nucleotides. This means that a restriction enzyme can be used to cut any length of DNA at those sites, and those sites only. Technically, this is extremely important. The human genome is around 3 billion nucleotides in length, and there is very little that can meaningfully be done with something this big if you can only chop it up *randomly* into manageable lengths. Being able to cut a genome or gene sequence predictably, precisely and repeatedly, makes a completely different kind of work possible. The discovery of the double helix was important because it initiated a course of discovery, and symbolically told the world that the mysteries of inheritance could be investigated with the available scientific tools. But the real revolution was a gift of bacterial biochemistry, and for that we owe the infamous gut bacterium *E.coli* and its relatives more thanks than they have ever received.

Contemporary genetic messages

A single technological step was the opener to the subsequent flood of techniques, applications, visionary scenarios and dreams that constitute contemporary gene technology. We live in a world becoming comfortable with the notion that a chemical is the repository of our biological history and our present day identity; that people are spoken into being by a chemical language, if you like. This is a radically different world from the pre-DNA one. It differs most obviously in what we can think of doing: diagnose diseases from blood samples or cheek scrapings before the symptoms appear, even before there is much of a body to embody the symptoms; identify the perpetrators and victims of crime from scraps of tissue; produce plants that are resistant or sensitive to chosen herbicides; produce, in one case, a rabbit that glows in the dark; envisage being able to treat genetic deficiencies by gene therapy, delivering compensatory genes as if they were aspirin.

The practical implementation of things like these has ethical and social impacts, and the next chapter considers some of them. But here I want to suggest that our world differs radically from the pre-DNA state not just in what we can think of *doing*, but in what we think we *are*. Basic genetic research has benefited from the availability of manipulatory tools, and there is now a level of knowledge about gene actions and the mechanisms of development and heredity that was unimaginable when I started out as a molecular biologist in the mid-1980s. The ideas, images and words used in the laboratory have made it to the world outside, so that genetics and molecular biology increasingly provide the framework for our cultural thoughts about what it means to be human. In this section I want to look at some of these contemporary genetic messages, considering what genetics tells us about things like human variation, the relationship between humans and between humans and other species, and the nature of human identity. Like the old joke where the pessimist perceives the glass as half empty while the optimist sees it as half full, how we interpret the genetic facts presented to us is a matter of choice. It is a moral, aesthetic and spiritual decision, which reflects fundamental things about our concepts of being human and being a person.

Human variation and relatedness

The story that genetics tells about human variation and relatedness is an ambiguous one. It says, for example, that (almost) every individual's genetic identity is unique, but at the same time virtually indistinguishable from that of every other person on the planet. Both these stories are true; it depends on how you look at it. Uniqueness is there because every time a human individual is conceived, a completely new genome is formed from the combination of the parental genetic components. With the exception of identical twins, no two individuals of the approximately 6 billion who currently inhabit the earth have genomes that are exactly the same.

But human genomes are made up of around 3 billion nucleotides, and only a surprisingly small number of nucleotides need to differ from one genome to another for each person to be unique. The draft human genome sequence announced in June 2000 indicated that around 99.9% of all nucleotides are the same in everyone. We are used to thinking of family members as being closely genetically related; now it appears that entire human communities, and what we used to think of as different human races, are not so different from a genomic point of view. Measuring genetic variation demonstrates in a striking way that the *average* genetic deviation between, say, blacks and whites is much smaller than the actual difference between any two individuals, irrespective of their ethnic origin. From this perspective, the old metaphor of the human family suddenly acquires a material basis.

Genetic relatedness does not stop at humans. The neo-Darwinian theory of evolution predicts that all living species are genetically related, and comparison of gene sequences from different species has shown exactly this. As we saw, the discovery of bacterial restriction enzymes made recombinant DNA technology possible. But the ability to use bacteria as a way of producing useful quantities of a specific human gene or the protein made from it, for example human insulin, depends on the remarkable fact that a gene from one organism will usually function in another. If the species difference is very great the gene might not be expressed very efficiently, and it might show up in odd places and at odd times, but essentially it will continue to produce the protein it codes for. If I could place a gene for a mouse hair protein into the cells of my scalp, I would probably end up with detectable levels of that mouse protein in my hair. (It wouldn't mean I had 'mouse hair'.) And the underlying reason is that humans and mice, along with fruit flies and bacteria and all other living things, share evolutionary ancestors, so that the hair protein gene in the mouse is almost the same as (or homologous to) the equivalent in humans. Fruit flies and bacteria don't have hair, which illustrates the side of the evolutionary story that is about difference and change, but they might well have genetic sequences which evolved over time into sequences associated with hair in mammals. The overall homology between the human and the mouse genome has been estimated at around 85%, between humans and chimpanzees around 98% (this is an average, as the percentage of homology varies from gene to gene).

Now relatedness of 98%, 85%, even 60%, is very close. Genetics extends the limits of 'who is related to me', widening the circle of relatedness to include not only other human beings, but other living organisms as well. In an important way, then, it reinforces some of our intuitions about the human community and the non-human world. This does not mean that genetics, by itself, tells us all we need to know about moral behaviour towards other species. There are questions genetics cannot yet, and may never be able to, answer (such as, if I am 90% genetically homologous to my cat, why am I writing this and not Winnie?). A more fundamental objection, however, is that there is something deeply wrong about basing our moral stance towards another entity – human or non-human – on whether or not it happens to possess the right set of chemicals. Moral relationships are often complicated; at times when they seem impossibly difficult, we need to guard against the temptation of thinking that reading our moral responsibilities in a chemical sequence offers a handy solution.

Genes in human development and disease

For historical and technical reasons, the study of human genetics is closely linked with medicine. Part of the historical connection is to do with the desire to repudiate the early, discredited link between human genetics and eugenics (improving the human 'stock') by focusing on *individual,* medical benefits as opposed to benefits to society. The technical reasons include the fact that genetic variation is detected by noticing physical change, and some of the most striking physical changes in humans are diseases. This connection means that much of what we know about genes in human life is actually about their role in disease, or in abnormal human development classed as disease or disability. It's worth asking whether human genetics, straying as it now does into the territory of 'normal' human characteristics and behaviour, has outgrown medicine – whether, in fact, the links between genetics and medicine persuade us too readily to think of aspects of human life, such as personality, as pathologies.

I said earlier that recombinant genetics has delivered a huge amount of experimental data about how genes behave. But this accumulation of data and details must be distinguished from a real understanding of the significance of genes in health and behaviour. Here our understanding is much more patchy, and what we do know suggests that the final story – if there ever is one – will be complex. Human characteristics, whether these are diseases or behavioural traits, appear to be influenced by a conglomeration of factors including a person's inherited constitution, the cellular and physiological milieu in which the genes are active, environmental factors such as diet and temperature, accidents of personal history such as relationships and experiences, and conscious choices. In the classic, well-characterised single gene (monogenic) diseases like Huntington's disease or cystic fibrosis the genetic contribution is clearly predominant. Even here, the embodied phenotype, in terms of things like the severity of the symptoms or the age at which a person develops the condition, can vary enough to suggest that more than one gene may be involved, and that there is at least some non-genetic component as well. And most of the human characteristics in which we are interested are already known to be more complex than monogenic disorders. Behavioural traits and the most common diseases such as heart disease, cancer and psychiatric disorders, result from the action of many genes (they are polygenic) and of other factors (they are multifactorial). So asthma is well-known to run in families, and the predisposition to having a hyperreactive respiratory tract is genetically linked. But actual asthmatic attacks are triggered by allergens like dust, environmental factors like cold air, internal physiological states like having a cold, and emotional stressors. By avoiding all the triggers (keeping my home totally free of dust and cat hair, never going out in winter, never catching cold, and never telephoning my mother), I could have all the genetic factors but never have an asthmatic attack.

Today, the most geneticists can say about the majority of characteristics is that they are influenced by both genetic and other factors, and that the relative contributions of these various influences cannot yet be quantified. This is an important point, because it means that the current focus on genetic causation for human ills is a matter of choice, and as with any selection something else gets neglected. It might be that other relevant factors are less open to manipulation than genetic ones, and therefore less interesting from the point of view of improving the human condition, but without investigating it is rather hard to tell. At the moment, we have at our disposal very powerful techniques of genetic analysis, which are generating a lot of interesting and useful data. But it's worth bearing in mind that just because these are the analytical techniques currently available, and even the ones that are most productive, they are not necessarily the ones that provide the best analyses.

Genes and human identity

This caveat is most relevant when we move towards integrating genetic understanding with our ideas about human identity. In comparison, comprehending how we get from the composition of the genome to what we observe as phenotypic variation is relatively straightforward. (Only relatively.) To the question, 'What makes you *you*?', I think most of us would bring in a diversity of elements: upbringing by our parents and families of origin, the work we do, our partners, children and friends, the communities we choose to live and work in, the bodies we were born with and the ones we now have, life-changing experiences, chance encounters, interests, beliefs, as well as genetics.

The problem is that this untidy conglomeration is not easily susceptible to the kind of analyses that our society currently finds most useful, which tend to be numerical ones. A technologically oriented society, and the bureaucracies that emerge in parallel, have a hankering for numbers; but how should I quantify meals with friends, a half-read newspaper article, or the fact that I went to Berlin and not Barcelona for New Year in 1990, as components of my identity? Part of the attraction of the genetic explanation for life, the universe and everything, is that it is readily quantifiable. The sizes of genes, the numbers of nucleotides that differ between genomes, or the proportions of the population carrying certain mutations, can be measured. There is also something appealing about being able to reduce all this complexity to a relatively small amount of coded information, which can then (in Walter Gilbert's notorious example) be put on a compact disk so that 'one will be able to pull a CD out of one's pocket and say, "Here is a human being; it's me!"' (Gilbert, 1993: 96).

If I believe that my individual identity derives predominantly from my genome, I can also hold that my identity is largely predictable and reproducible, regardless of any influences from environment or context. Identity becomes a discrete component, which can in some way be stored in little nuggets of DNA. Furthermore, the picture I have of the steps between genome and individual identity will affect the *nature* of the individuality that I think exists at the end of the day.

Only the most hardline determinist would say out loud that human identity is determined solely by genes, or that environmental factors and free will play no role in it. Statements about gene action are always qualified with a nod to the importance of non-genetic factors, and these qualifications are sincerely meant. Nevertheless, the language used by many molecular or evolutionary biologists, and by much of the media, has a way of unconsciously conveying a different message. So, for example, human characteristics are described as being *determined* by genes but only *influenced* by non-genetic factors: 'The general colour of your skin is genetically determined...many characteristics may be influenced by the environment as well as by genes...altering environmental influences...can markedly influence the course of development...' (Bains, 1987: 13). If these are the words and images used then whatever the overt message, the flavour of determinism will linger.

Whether or not I find a deterministic approach to genetics congenial is a matter of personal preference. What I want to point out here is that, even within the scientific community, the conventional model of gene action is being revised, not for reasons of ideological distaste but because it fails to explain the data. New experimental evidence has challenged the classic concept of a gene as an uninterrupted stretch of DNA coding for a single protein. Biologists and philosophers of science are developing models that relate gene expression to the organism as a whole, and to the processes through which organisms develop and persist. For example, one model, the process molecular gene concept (Neumann-Held, 2001), defines a gene not as a length of DNA but as a recurring *process*, in the context of which DNA sequences are given meaning. In the systems theory approach, DNA is looked on as one part of an interrelated 'system' of parts and processes, which includes the cell and its components as well as features of the environment.

Models that relate gene expression to the whole organism, to processes and context, are necessary simply in order to fit the biological data. At the same time they enlarge our repertoire of ways of interpreting how genetic information and identity are related. These models offer a different picture of identity: not something encapsulated in the genome and predictably and reproducibly expressed, but emerging from the interplay of various genetic elements and concrete environmental circumstances, the unpredictable result of diverse developmental pathways and histories of interaction, transient and responsive, and fully interpretable only in terms of particular conditions and relationships (Rehmann-Sutter, 1999).

I mention these new models of gene action less because I think they are superior to the alternatives, than simply to show that they exist. Even within strictly scientific parameters, there is more than one way of understanding the evidence in terms both of biological processes and of what it means for our concept of human persons. Irrespective of whether we think science is morally neutral or value laden, genetic theories of human development, once they get out of the lab – as they always do – ultimately become ethical statements. The theory of human development that we choose has a way of reflecting our beliefs about human nature, and so of shaping how these beliefs are acted out in real-life situations of personal, political and social consequence. These consequences are the subject of the next chapter.

3

ETHICAL ISSUES IN GENE TECHNOLOGY

> boss my interest in science
> is keen but my
> sympathy with scientists is
> declining very rapidly the
> more i see of
> them the less i
> want them to see
> me...
> what is sport to
> you old fellow is
> death to us insects morality
> is all in the point
> of view...
>
> *Don Marquis, archyology*

In this chapter I want to look at ethical issues in gene technology. The constraints of space mean I cannot cover any area in detail, or give predictions or prescriptions about how particular issues should be dealt with. Detail may even be unhelpful in an overview of a technology where the rapid pace of change affects the associated ethical issues as well. At the time of writing, stem cell cloning is particularly high on the ethical agenda; but who can predict how long it will stay there, what sort of resolution people will eventually come to, and what will replace it as the next big thing?

Instead I will give a broad outline of a few major ethical questions. Some concern human beings, some our relationship with other species on the planet, and some seem to touch both. In each case, I will highlight what I see as the main moral difficulties associated with them, and why. (And in each case this reflects my own point of view, so that other people might well pick out different aspects as being most problematic.) Finally, I will try to identify broader themes that are discernible within these particular concrete examples, and that seem to be common to more than one issue. Spotting common themes in apparently disparate issues can be a good way to reveal what really unnerves us; a starting point, at least, for engaging with novel and intractable problems. It may turn out that addressing these broader themes proves more powerful than directly tackling the individual issues in genetic ethics.

Human beings
Acquiring and using genetic information
Even before the Human Genome Project (HGP) began to map and sequence examples of the human genetic constitution, much was already known about various genes, especially disease-related ones. In many cases it was possible to find out whether a person's genome contained an *allele* (a particular gene form) associated with a condition. The first draft of the human genome was published in July 2000, but the work of completing and then analysing the information will continue for years to come. The development of technologies to allow rapid (and cheap) screening on an industrial scale means that acquiring and using genetic information is also becoming easier. In the past, genetic testing was generally only offered to people who knew from their family history that they might have inherited a particular condition, or to a person already showing symptoms. In the future, genetic testing is likely to be applied in the form of widespread screening of individuals or groups with no previous family history or symptoms.

Genetic testing and screening of adults raises questions about *confidentiality* and *access* to genetic information. For example, if one member of a family has been tested for a heritable condition, do other members – who might want to know about their chances of having the gene or the disease, but also want to avoid being tested themselves – have a right to access the information? One reason to avoid being tested is that having information means you can be asked (or pressured) to disclose the result, or just the fact that you have been tested, to bodies outside the family. These might be insurers, for example, or employers. There has already been considerable public discussion about the legitimacy of insurance companies making use of individual genetic information. While the insurance business tends to argue that genetic data are no different from the medical information it is already allowed to use, many people *do* feel that genes are different. Genes are directly 'about' other people as well as the individual seeking insurance. Furthermore, the simple presence of a gene may not result in any effects that could be of use in making actuarial calculations. And (as described in chapter 2) our understanding of how genes work is currently so basic that there is a very real danger of grossly misinterpreting the significance of genetic data.

Collecting and analysing genetic information introduces the potential for discriminating against people who possess genes associated with diseases, or even behaviours, and since having the gene is not the same thing as having a condition, it could be particularly damaging to people who carry a gene but are not symptomatic. Genetic information could be misused, not just by insurance companies, although they have attracted most attention so far, but also by employers, the police, schools and universities, the military – anyone, in fact, up to and including our friends and neighbours. Human beings are disturbingly good at finding reasons to despise other people, and possession of gene variants is unlikely to be an exception.

This could easily extend to groups as well as individuals. For example, the emerging field of *pharmacogenomics* attempts to correlate the genetic profiles of particular population groups with responses to medication. People vary hugely in how they respond to a drug, and much (though not all) of this is thought to be due to genetic variation in the way the body handles incoming chemicals, like aspirin. The pharmaceutical industry is particularly interested in being able to 'tailor' drug treatment to patients according to their genetic make-up. Some responses, however, are found more commonly in particular ethnic groups than in others, and this raises the concern that pharmacogenomics will turn into just another way of exercising discrimination (for example, if pharmaceutical companies neglect to develop drugs that are more effective in blacks than in whites on the grounds that, on average, whites will be better able to pay for them).

As well as thinking about other people's access to our genetic information, we also need to think about our own. Is it necessarily good for me to find out I have a condition, or predisposition to a condition, especially if nothing much can be done about it? There are certainly diseases where knowledge of a predisposition can be useful, such as cancers, where regular screening can detect early tumours. But in most cases our ability to detect genetic associations far outstrips our ability to cure or ameliorate a disease, and this means we have to think hard about whether knowledge, of itself, is a good thing. At an individual level, the answer to this is personal and quite unpredictable. Some people want to know everything and then deal with it, others would rather not know if they don't have to, and still others (like me) change their minds when it comes to the crunch. On a collective level, the answer reflects the tension between individual rights and the responsibilities of a society to all its constituents. A person might indeed *want* information, but a state-funded healthcare system, where effectiveness is assessed as the cost per patient, might not feel obliged to offer testing when, from *its* point of view, there would be no resulting economic benefit.

All of these issues are connected with the so far unresolved question of who, if anyone, really 'owns' genetic information.

On the whole, I think my personal, embodied medical history of vaccinations, infections, accidents and so on, is mine alone. But my *genetic* story overlaps with the genetic stories of my whole family, my community, and the (several) ethnic groups to which I belong. So to what extent can I claim that genetic information belongs to me?

Prenatal genetic testing and screening

Genetic testing can also be done *prenatally*, and the diagnosis of a condition in an embryo or foetus presents a different set of problems. As with adult diagnosis, the ability to identify genes is much greater than our ability to treat or cure. The difference in the case of the foetus is the option of abortion. In most western societies abortion is legal under certain circumstances, indicating an acknowledgement by society that sometimes termination of pregnancy may be the right (or least wrong) thing to do; and the 'certain circumstances' usually include pregnancies where the foetus is likely to have some kinds of disability. We accept – up to a point – that a woman or a couple have the right to decide not just what happens to her body, but what kind of child they want to have.

Abortion and the status of the foetus are important moral questions in themselves, and not ones to address here. I want only to point out that when genetic testing is used to characterise the unborn child, we face additional ethical questions. Some of these are genuinely new but, as often seems to happen in gene technology, others look more like ones we have just managed to avoid up till now. One major difficulty is interpreting the genetic information that becomes available. As we saw in chapter 2, most characteristics result from the combination of genetic and non-genetic factors, with every characteristic perhaps having its own unique package of influences. It is not often possible to predict exactly what the physical manifestation of a genetic abnormality will be, let alone the woollier things like how a person or a family will cope.

If, through prenatal genetic and other diagnosis, we are morally and legally permitted to decide what is an 'acceptable' foetus (and some people would query that), what criteria should we use? In the past the criteria have been to do with disease and disability; they have included things like whether suffering is involved, and the effect of a disease or disability on the individual, the family, and (more questionably) society as a whole. But genetic information is not just about cystic fibrosis or diabetes; it is also about hair colour and height, it might be about shyness and sexual desire, it could imaginably have something to say about career choice and religious belief. (While some genetically influenced characteristics clearly do affect career choice – colourblind males should not become pilots – I think that *direct* gene influences, a 'gene for' librarianship or Quakerism, are unlikely. But in reality no one knows for sure.) There is a risk that, gradually, everything that can be shown to have a genetic link will start to be seen as a problem, whether or not it is disabling or causes any kind of suffering. Should we perhaps be asking whether genetic information actually does offer the right criteria, or whether it just happens to be there, abundant and increasingly easy to get hold of?

Gene therapy and genetic enhancement

Much the same questions arise when we think beyond simple testing, to the actual *manipulation* of the genes in therapy or enhancement. In gene therapy, the idea is to replace a variant gene that produces a malfunctioning protein, or no protein at all, with a gene or gene fragment that provides the missing function. In *somatic gene therapy*, the missing protein would be replaced in the affected tissues of an adult or child – for example, in the muscles of someone with muscular dystrophy – and only the individual being treated would be affected by the genetic change.

Largely because of this restriction, somatic gene therapy is often considered to be fairly unproblematic in ethical terms. The main areas of concern are less to do with the manipulation of the genome than the morality of offering an experimental therapy to desperately sick people, or the diversion of finite healthcare resources to develop a therapy that will probably only ever be available to the well-off.

Germ line gene therapy differs from somatic gene therapy in that the missing protein would be replaced in all or most of the cells of a very early embryo, including the sex (or germ) cells. Therefore any genetic change would not be restricted to that person but could be passed on to his or her descendants. Because this would mean imposing an irrevocable change and unpredictable consequences on future generations who have no way of giving their consent, most bioethicists consider germ line gene therapy not to be morally permissible (although there are some who disagree).

At heart, both forms of gene therapy (together with *preimplantation genetic diagnosis*, which involves in vitro screening and selection of embryos before they are implanted into the uterus as part of IVF) pose the same question as prenatal genetic diagnosis, but – crucially – without the complicating factor of abortion: If we can manipulate the genome to ameliorate or cure disease, in existing individuals and/or their descendants, should we do it? The issue here is the choice of the kind of people we want to have (which raises the question of who 'we' are in this context), irrespective of other, important questions about the right to life or the moral status of the foetus or embryo. The argument that irreversible genetic changes should never be imposed on future, possibly unwilling, individuals, seems a very strong one. But suppose one day we identify a genetic modification that gives resistance to AIDS, one that appears not to have any undesirable side-effects, and that in order to be effective has to be introduced very early in embryonic development. What to do then? Hypothetical examples like this suggest the absolute wrongness of germ line manipulation is not always clear-cut.

In discussing genetic manipulation, many ethicists have attempted to draw a line between *therapeutic interventions* – 'true' gene therapy, involving the treatment of disease – and *enhancements* – such as increasing height, or boosting memory. This is often described as the difference between making people better, and making better people. Because the technology used for both gene therapy and genetic enhancement will, most likely, be exactly the same, differences in the techniques themselves cannot indicate the limits to manipulating the human genome to 'improve' it. (This is worth keeping in mind as a general point about technology – that it's unwise to rely on the constraints of technique to provide ethical boundaries as well.)

We will probably have to look beyond biology, and beyond our ideas about what is 'natural', to locate any ethical limits to modifying the human body. For one thing, concepts of what is natural for a body or person vary enormously over time, between cultures and simply according to familiarity (as a deaf person I find it unnatural, bordering on perverse, that some people want to have conversations in the dark). For another, in practical terms what counts as a therapy in present day society has less to do with biology than with who has agreed to pay for it. There is a further difficulty in trying to distinguish cleanly between therapy and enhancement, which is that the two categories only appear clear if somewhere in between them is a line labelled 'normality' – so that bringing someone up to this line is restoring them to normality, in other words it is therapy, but taking them beyond this line is enhancement. I think most of us would acknowledge that getting general agreement on exactly what this normality should look like, would not be easy. But we would also agree that regulating genetic interventions is a good idea. To produce legislation that permits therapy but not enhancement, we will have to describe –

perhaps in law – what this norm consists of. And I think our society's tolerance for difference, not great at the best of times, would be weakened by the provision of a codification of human normality. Many of those concerned about the rights of disabled people worry that a society in which normality has become defined, especially in genetic terms, will inevitably show less acceptance of deviations from the norm.

Reproductive and therapeutic cloning

In a very few years, cloning has moved from being a staple of science fiction films to a bleating reality in the shape of Dolly, the first cloned sheep. Since Dolly was born several other mammalian species have been successfully cloned. Technically, cloning is a high-tech form of cell biology rather than a genetic technology and it need not involve any manipulation of the genetic material. Nevertheless, cloning can be combined with the techniques of genetic manipulation to produce large numbers of identical, and genetically altered, animals. It therefore shares some ethical issues, and raises others of its own.

A distinction must be drawn between different kinds of cloning. The term 'cloning' in itself means nothing more esoteric than the production of genetically identical copies, which is what is done whenever we take a cutting and grow a new geranium from it. Molecular biologists also refer to cloning or subcloning genes, meaning isolating genes in a form in which they can be copied in large amounts for study or practical use.

Neither of these, of course, is what most people think of in connection with cloning, which is the creation of genetically identical copies of a sheep – or a person. This is *reproductive cloning*, the reproduction of an organism. The ethical debate roused by the arrival of Dolly focused on the possible consequences of human reproductive cloning. Worldwide, the current consensus of opinion seems to be that cloning a person would be transgressing a significant moral boundary.

A number of reasons have been put forward to explain why human cloning is morally wrong. One of the first arguments to be raised was that it damages human dignity or reduces the value of the individual. I know some Friends will be disappointed when I say it, but to be honest I don't find this argument very convincing. The problem is that I don't see how producing a genetic copy shows disrespect for human personhood, *unless* you believe that personhood is defined by an individual's genetic makeup. If personhood, individuality, identity are constituted by lots of other factors as well as genetic ones, then a clone would be at least as much an individual as a twin is, and perhaps more so.

This does not mean that I think human cloning is acceptable, because there are more convincing objections. There are legitimate questions to be asked, for example, about the motives of anyone wanting a clone instead of reproducing in more tried and tested ways. In addition to those who are, for whatever reason, infertile, cloning might be attractive to people who actually want a copy of themselves rather than a child that is a mixture of their own and someone else's genomes. In these cases, it has been argued that wanting a child by cloning is an unworthy desire. Unlike the usual way of becoming parents, it does not accept the child as a unique individual that has its own 'freedom to be'; it treats the child as a product to be designed at will. (Similar arguments are used against genetic testing or manipulation of embryos; cloning is seen as an extreme case of the same trend towards 'designer babies'.)

The possibility that parental motives for cloning might be grounds for disrespect or damage is worrying. There is a very real danger of turning children into products, and there are real issues to do with the limits of parental control and our acceptance of randomness. *But these issues have always been there.* This may be another area where we are being forced to think about difficulties we have so far avoided. Perhaps our ideal of parenthood, and of the motivations for becoming parents, should be looked at more critically. People decide to reproduce for all kinds of reasons, some of which are flagrantly selfish, and some parents clearly do treat their 'normally produced' children as commodities. Our worry that cloning or genetic selection allows parents to commodify their offspring, or to control reproduction to an unacceptable degree, may actually be a way of allowing us to express our unease about behaviour that, in reality, is already only too common.

The risk to the potential clones is another real problem. In all the animal species where it has so far been achieved, cloning is still technically difficult and inefficient. The rate of failures (clones that do not develop) is very high, and it also looks as if the cloned animals that do make it into the world often have developmental disorders of varying severity. This kind of damage might be ethically acceptable in animals (although many people would disagree). But most of us would find it completely unacceptable to refine the procedure of human cloning, *knowing* that it would inevitably mean creating severely damaged individuals in the process.

Even if reproductive human cloning were efficient and safe, a further issue would be the kind of life a clone might face. Would a cloned person encounter prejudice or hostility, and would knowing about their unusual genesis cause psychological damage? These are valid worries, although how unique they are to cloning is debatable. It is worth reflecting that the fear of discrimination is a greater condemnation of our communities than it is of cloning.

My biggest reservation about reproductive cloning remains the question of priorities. Cloning may help people to have children where they otherwise could not, but is this a strong enough rationale, given the problems it could cause, and given that the time and money devoted to developing the technology would provide healthcare to more people than will ever benefit from cloning? It is not an easy thing to say to people desperate for a child, but our current almost unconditional commitment to all the reproductive technologies (not just cloning) may simply place too high a value on 'getting a baby'.

In *therapeutic cloning* the idea is to produce tissues to treat disease or damage – for example, brain tissue to replace neurons damaged by neurodegenerative disorders – but to avoid the problems of rejection that arise when organs from another individual are used, by cloning a person's own tissue. In both reproductive and therapeutic cloning, the nucleus of a cell from one of the body's tissues is inserted into an unfertilised egg which has had its own nucleus removed. The result, if all goes well, is an embryo. The difference in therapeutic cloning is that instead of going on to produce a whole new cloned individual, the aim is to obtain embryonic *stem cells* with the potential to develop into the tissues required in therapy. Currently the most reliable and prolific sources of stem cells are embryos, or cell lines derived from embryo tissues.

These embryos can be produced by the cloning technique described above in situations where rejection is a problem, but otherwise (in research, for example) any embryo will do. They might also come from abortions or miscarriages, or be 'excess' embryos produced in IVF treatment. This poses obvious questions about the ethics of using, or perhaps even creating, embryos with the sole aim of extracting cells from them to benefit someone else. And since, at least as the technology now stands, therapeutic cloning would create a demand for unfertilised human eggs while stem cell therapy needs embryonic tissue, a black market could emerge that would preferentially exploit the poorest and most vulnerable women worldwide.

At the time of writing, therapeutic cloning and the use of embryonic stem cells are hot issues, and regulations vary from country to country. In 2001, for example, the United Kingdom decided to permit surplus embryos from IVF to be used in stem cell research, either directly or to establish cultured stem cell lines; shortly after, the United States ruled that federal funds could *not* support research that involved creating new stem cell lines; and meanwhile Switzerland forbids embryonic tissue to be used for research, but permits the import of stem cell lines.

To me the issues in reproductive cloning are more complex (and to be honest, more interesting) than those of therapeutic cloning and stem cells. While reproductive cloning, as we saw, raises a wide range of questions about identity and social behaviour, opinions about the morality of therapeutic cloning are dominated by controversy over the moral status of the embryo. Just because therapeutic cloning involves a less multifaceted ethical situation, however, does not mean it is any easier to resolve; years of discussion about the morality of abortion have demonstrated the impossibility of reconciling everyone's beliefs about exactly what can and cannot be done to and with embryos.

Other species

The end of the last century saw a rising awareness of environmental issues, and most of us are now conscious of the ecological and moral importance of nonhuman species. For some people, the genetic manipulation of nonhuman animals and plants is even *more* contentious than anything to do with human beings, because animals or plants cannot give their consent to the genetic manipulations, which are usually done to increase their utility for us. At the other end of the spectrum are people who see no difference between traditional selective breeding techniques and genetic manipulation as practised in laboratories today. And in between these extremes lies a range of people who are less exercised by the overall concept of *exploitation* but feel that inflicting *genetic changes* on other species as part of our exploitation takes us onto a new level of ethical responsibility.

What makes a *genetic* change so different? Some people are concerned that the introduced genetic modifications will cause suffering to the animals (they see it primarily as an issue of animal welfare). Others are troubled by altering what they see as an essential part of the species identity. This is not the same as an individual identity, which carries more weight in the objections to human genetic manipulation. The difference between individual and species identity is probably why the idea of cloning people is generally (not universally) considered far more offensive than cloning animals. Nevertheless, in many people's eyes the genome holds something essential to the identity and integrity of a species, and changing it is problematic for reasons that may be to do with animal rights, usurping God's creative power, or transgressing natural laws.

Patenting

The patenting of genetically modified organisms has served as a focus of moral concern in this area. It is also legally complex, and national and international regulations are subject to revision, and so I make no attempt here to consider it in depth – there are other sources (see back of the book) for those who want more detail.

The main argument in favour of protecting intellectual property (patenting) concerns justice. Defenders of patenting intellectual property say that it is only fair for an inventor to receive the benefits of his or her invention. Scaling up from the lone inventor, biotechnological and pharmaceutical research involves such massive investment of time and money that it needs the kind of time-limited commercial protection provided by patenting. The proponents of patenting focus on this single issue of the right to protect an invention.

Because the opponents of patenting have a wider spread of concerns, they have found it harder to articulate them in such a focused way. They too are concerned about justice: in this case, the fact that the countries richest in patentable genetic resources are in the poor South, and are the most vulnerable to exploitation by the North/West. They worry about the potential for intellectual property rights to consolidate the growing economic and political power of transnational companies. They may also have more metaphysical questions around the ethics of 'patenting life'. Here, the major concerns may be that allowing the patenting of genetically modified *living organisms* means they are being treated as commodities, and that this insidiously undermines our respect for life. Or the question may be whether it is ethical to patent *genetic information* (an increasing number of patent applications are made for gene sequences or fragments, rather than for any living organism). The fact that this question is raised confirms that many people consider genetic information to have a unique status, related to, but not exactly the same as, life itself, and therefore requiring a special kind of treatment. The existing system of patents was devised to offer commercial protection for inventors of objects; it has the flavour not just of ownership but of invention/creation, and this may be inappropriate for living things, or even genes, whatever quirky relation genetic information has to 'life itself'.

At the time of writing patents have been applied for and granted on several thousand genetically manipulated organisms, or the gene sequences they carry. Public protest has not blocked the issuing of patents, but it has effectively brought the issue onto the political agenda. Several national and European regulatory or advisory bodies are working on proposals for alternatives to the current patenting system that would protect inventors' rights as well as respect the dignity of creation, or the rights of indigenous peoples to their traditional knowledge if it turns out to be commercially exploitable. The regulatory and public discussion shows that patenting cannot be treated as an abstract ethical problem detached from the social and political context in which it takes place. Concerns about the power of transnationals, for instance, cannot be adequately addressed *solely* by changes in patent law (although they might be a step in the right direction).

Natural/unnatural

The distinction between *natural and unnatural* is at the heart of many objections to genetic manipulation, but it is not as straight-forward as first appears. Making the distinction takes for granted that we all know what is natural and what isn't, and that we can always tell when something is one or the other. Often this boils down to assuming that 'natural' is whatever the nonhuman world gets up to if left to its own devices. But the complexity of the rela-tionship between human activities and the environment means that very often, none of these assumptions hold up. Are the South Downs natural? Do urban foxes behave naturally, and if not, what *are* they doing?

Some broader themes
Human being and human nature

One clearly emerging theme, which has important ethical impli-cations, is that genetic ideas affect our understanding of what it means to be human. This is not unprecedented. History suggests that our notions of who and what we are, in communities and as persons, change as old ideas fade and new ones take over. What may be unique about this 'genetic event' is the speed with which data are being generated and ideas transported beyond the pro-fessional domain to change the lives of the rest of us. Perhaps we have also reached a point in the lifecycle of a global pluralist society when we are more conscious than before, not simply of our need to make sense of our lives, but of the need to make coherent sense of many different ways of living. The project now is to inte-grate genetic ideas about what makes a person into our traditional ideas, without losing touch with those older concepts where they remain true for us.

This will be especially challenging when and if genetics produces compelling evidence for a significant genetic component to aspects of human *behaviour*, rather than disease. (Some biologists are sceptical that this will ever happen, others look at the data and believe it already has. A lot depends on what you define as significant.) It is possible we may have particular difficulty if we find evidence of a genetic element to human behaviours we approve of. It's one thing to absolve ourselves of human *vices* with the thought that we are genetically or evolutionarily programmed to have them, quite another to suggest that we can't claim the credit for good behaviour either, if our *virtues* are genetic too. As I discussed in chapter 2, it is unlikely that any genetic influence on human characteristics will be all or nothing, but it will take substantial mental and spiritual self-discipline to avoid taking the easy road towards either of these extremes.

Concepts of human being, beliefs about human nature and what part genes play in it, all have ethical consequences. If my identity derives in some way from my genome, then the details of the steps involved in getting from genome to me will influence, at least in part, who or what I am at the end of the process. The most commonly presented, popular picture of gene action is a *deterministic* one that runs linearly from gene through protein to organism and identity. In chapter 2 I mentioned some alternatives, and it is important to keep an eye on the models being developed, and how they leach into the public mind and colour our thinking. How we see our identity as being formed influences our concept of ourselves as moral agents, and this has implications for issues of moral responsibility, autonomy, authority, relationship and so on. If I think that the procedure by which individuals are made is a kind of 'molecular Meccano' (Bains 1987: 7), or that genes 'spell out a recipe...for building, growing and running a living human body' (a statement in the brochure of the Centre for Life, Newcastle, 1999), then I am likely to hold opinions about choice, free will, and effective intervention in human affairs that reflect this belief. Constructing my ideas about human identity on this foundation might make me more willing to think that, owing to the direct causal relationship between the two, by changing our genes we can change our identities. Moreover, since in this model all other factors – internal or external environmental influences, for example, or personal decisions – are secondary to the genetic ones, then changing our genes would also appear to be the *most effective* way of changing our identities.

Conversely, if I see identity as an emergent property shaped by other forces as well as the genome, or as a purely social construct, or as instantaneous and transient rather than continuous and stable, then in each case I am likely to hold different opinions about the effectiveness of social reform in improving human behaviour, or the moral culpability of a murderer. Faith in the direct one-to-one mapping between genes and identity lies behind some of the strong reactions to the idea of human cloning. The argument that it is a violation of human dignity to attempt to reproduce an individual identity relies on the assumption that by replicating a specific genome, we are replicating a specific identity as well.

Variation and normality

Another recurrent theme concerns concepts of normality/abnormality, of the source and meaning of disability, and whether human variation causes suffering.

Molecular genetics has a distinctive take on normality and abnormality, and some of this is being transferred to the public domain along with genetic ideas. By identifying genetic abnormalities, an increasingly detailed picture of the abnormal is assembled. But this is done with the purpose of providing a picture of the normal. The aim is not really to define abnormality (disease), but normality (health) *in absentia*. Tactically this simplifies things a great deal. Defining normality as the absence of certain abnormalities means we define it without having to ask whether in fact this is a meaningful or feasible thing to do. The model of identity derived from deterministic genetics says that normality is something that can be clearly distinguished from abnormality, *because* 'the' normal genome can be clearly distinguished from abnormal ones, and because the genome gives rise in a predictable fashion to identity. This ability to turn frustratingly woolly concepts of health and normality into something more concrete is one reason why the deterministic model of gene action is so attractive. Normality and abnormality no longer have to be assessed subjectively; they become gene variants that can be identified by the right genetic test.

The sequencing of the human genome has changed the way we think about biological and medical norms. It reinforces the idea that there is a single normal human genome rather than numerous normalities, that this canonical gene sequence is equivalent to the embodied human, and that once we have sequenced the genome we will be able to 'read off' directly the norms of human embodiment. By extension, a genome that deviates from the genomic norm becomes a defective genome that generates an abnormal embodiment.

I said earlier that gene therapy and preimplantation genetic diagnosis are likely to make it possible to select a child's characteristics without the 'complicating factor' of abortion. More directly than before, then, we are confronted with what we really think about diversity in embodiment and ability. Until recently the dominant model for understanding varied embodiment, and imagining what if anything to do about it, was provided by the medical model which sees disability largely as disease, degeneration, defect or deficit. Dissatisfied with the limitations of a purely medical perspective for comprehending the experiential reality of disability, the disability movement has proposed alternative models under the broad heading of social models of disability. Their essential criticism of the medical model is that it wrongly locates the 'problem' of disability purely in biological difference and neglects the contribution of social, economic and environmental factors.

When trying to integrate genetics into ideas about normality, it is helpful to be as clear as possible about where biological fact becomes interpretation. Genetic information about human variation, for example, can be used without necessarily setting normal and abnormal in opposition to each other. Variant embodiments might be characterised solely by medical or even genetic criteria, but could still be interpreted as variations on a theme, or on several themes. Seeing them as deviations from a standard is an interpretative *choice*, and is not intrinsic to the data provided by molecular biology.

Guidance from nature

A large part of the urge to make the natural/unnatural distinction, mentioned earlier, is the hope that nature will provide moral guidance. Using nature as a spiritual indicator has a long history, and some aspects of natural theology (traditionally, the rationally obtained knowledge of God), and of the Catholic natural law tradition (which looks for analogy between creation and the kingdom of God), are relevant here. The history is not straightforward, and mainstream Christian theology oscillates between seeing nature, God's creation, as an ideal of the good, or as a distraction that must be subdued to achieve goodness.

The popularity of taking nature as a *moral* guide is, I think, more recent and is related to the loss of credibility of organised religion. In an increasingly secularised society, people use nature to replace a God they feel embarrassed to talk about or no longer find to be a useful explanatory concept. It's interesting that in many debates about gene technology, for example, the words 'God' and 'nature/Gaia' could be used interchangeably without substantially affecting what is said (and often nature seems to attract considerably more moral credibility than God). Nature is often personified, as if 'she' has a will and desires of 'her' own ('nature knows best'), while the suffering that was once described as the result of sin, our failure to live as God intended, is now blamed on human interference in the natural balance, the failure to live as nature intends. The assumption that whatever is natural is also good, or at least preferable to the humanly produced alternative, is a powerful rhetorical device. It has the advantage of providing an apparently clear answer to many of our ethical queries (if it doesn't happen in nature then it can't be right). And if nature is currently 'standing in for' God, it is easy to see why nature has to provide ethical guidance, just as God traditionally has.

I want to be clear that I am not arguing against attempts to understand creation in order to discern morally good ways of interacting with it, or good ways of being human. But the interpretation must be a sensitive and subtle one that brings in many different objective and subjective kinds of knowledge. Taking a selective picture of nature and using it uncritically is not only potentially misleading. In the extreme, it can be just another form of abuse: exploiting nature to satisfy our own craving for certainty, forgetting that the natural world is there for itself. It is not there to tell us what to do.

Global justice

Many of us share a concern about the *just distribution of resources* in healthcare. This affects all aspects of genetic medicine, where the techniques are high-tech and expensive, and likely to remain so. How can their development be justified, when in the world as a whole most people do not have access to the most basic level of healthcare? Some of its advocates have suggested that, eventually, gene technology will become cheap enough to benefit people outside the rich North/West, but so far there is no evidence of this happening. In any case it raises its own ethical questions about the use that might be made of genetic techniques in different cultural contexts – prenatal diagnosis to select against girl children, for example, which already happens in many countries. There are plausible scenarios by which genetic manipulation *could* be used to help the poorer world, such as producing disease-resistant crops, or vaccines that do not have to be kept cold. But even its advocates acknowledge that in a minimally regulated, globalised free market, gene technology is more likely to increase the economic and social polarisation between those who can afford it and those who can't. This would not be unique to gene technology, of course, and once again our criticism of genetics forces us to scrutinise other areas of life just as critically.

Discerning the real issues

Threading through all these problems and themes, I think, is the task of discerning the real issues. What at first sight seems like a disastrous consequence of the use of gene technology can sometimes, on examination, be revealed as coming from a difficulty located elsewhere. When we look at prenatal genetic diagnosis, for example, our dread of discrimination against people with variant embodiments has obviously not arisen with genetics. It can be traced back to intolerance within our communities, and beyond that perhaps to individual and collective insecurities about one's own identity. Similarly, some of our concerns about patenting can more properly be located in our fear that the unprecedented financial and political power of transnational companies allows them to operate outside all moral constraints.

In both of these examples, the real problem is not genetic

manipulation, but what happens when the technology is put to work in the context of particular social values. This is an exceptionally obvious point to labour, but it is important and worth repeating for a number of reasons. One is that we are unlikely to solve any problem if we are unable to discern and address the real cause(s), if we are distracted by a convenient scapegoat. Another is that, if we genuinely want to evaluate gene technology's potential for good and evil, we need clarity about the social and political frameworks that shape how it is used, and insight into how these frameworks might need to be transformed to ensure the technology is used well. And finally, a more sensitive understanding of our fears might have a diagnostic function. It could indicate problem areas we did not know were there, or did not realise were so important to us, but that we urgently need to look at.

Once the real issues have been identified, of course, we still have to address them. In the next chapter I want to consider that good ways of doing scientific research, and of implementing science in the world, can be suggested by a particularly evocative and contentious metaphor: science as playing.

4

AT PLAY IN THE FIELDS OF THE LORD [1]

Then I was at his side each day,
his darling and delight,
playing in his presence continually.
Proverbs 8:30 (New English Bible)

play, vb. 1. To occupy oneself in (a sport or diversion)
... 4. to behave carelessly, esp. in a way that is
unconsciously cruel or hurtful. 5. to perform or act
the part... 7. to have the ability to perform on (a
musical instrument).
*(Four of the 18 meanings of the verb to play
listed in* Collins Concise Dictionary *1988)*

Playing God

In this chapter I want to consider science as a form of play.
Many Friends will find this initially off-putting. We tend not to
think of playfulness as appropriate behaviour for adults (especially, perhaps, adult Quakers). Play does not seem serious enough
to be used in connection with a serious activity like science, and
its potentially very un-playful consequences.

I began thinking about play and science when I noticed how
frequently the public discussion of genetic manipulation turned to
the idea that we, or scientists on our behalf, are 'playing God'. I'm
not sure when the motif was first used, although June Goodfield
quotes a microbiologist at the Asilomar conference of 1975 as
saying, 'Nature does not need to be legislated. But playing God
does' (Goodfield: 1977). The notion of playing God is an interesting and complicated one. In the context of gene technology it is

---

1 The title of this chapter comes from the novel *At Play in the Fields of the Lord*, by Peter Matthieson,
which describes the impact of western missionaries on South American indigenous people.

invariably used negatively, which is interesting since *to play* can mean *to perform*, and performing the actions of God in the world is surely what we all have to do. The implication in 'playing God' is that we are playing an *illegitimate* role, going much further than we should. Playing *God* indicates the kind of power that people think genetic manipulation gives us, and the impact of the interventions that could be made. 'Playing' here has the second of the dictionary meanings given above: behaving thoughtlessly and irresponsibly, mucking about. 'Playing God' suggests that gene technology confers the ability to do things that previously were strictly within God's province, but without also giving us the divine perspective to do it wisely.

I understood these anxieties and to an extent I shared them. Gradually, though, I became uneasy, and the motif of 'playing God' became so problematic for me that very early in this period of exploration I decided to abandon it. For one thing, the accusation that someone else is playing God establishes a sweeping claim to the moral high ground, one that makes it hard for any other claims to be heard. For another, the theological power of the accusation allows us to avoid looking closely at what we actually mean by it, even before considering whether the accusation is justifiable. If playing God means adapting the world and ourselves according to our desires, then human beings have been doing it ever since one of our brighter ancestors noticed that wearing animal fur made winter a lot more comfortable, not to say survivable. If it means using our creative abilities in illegitimate ways, or in ways inappropriate for humans, then we need to be clearer about the limits of legitimacy and appropriateness (particularly in a pluralistic society with a diversity of opinion about the nature or existence of the God being played). In this sense being human and playing God becomes a question of degree. In reality none of us can be sure where the cutoff point lies, and using unexamined phrases may do nothing more than provide a cover for our uncertainty.

I was nagged by the feeling that science and play do, somehow, go together. It was at this point that I was reminded of the appearance of Wisdom, or Sophia, in the book of Proverbs, where she is described as playing at the side of God and delighting God with her play. I was not sure how Wisdom could have anything to do with play, but it reinforced my intuition that the link between science and play is a good one, and that understanding more about it might disclose something about ways of doing science.

According to the *Bloomsbury Dictionary of Word Origins*:

> the origins of play are obscure. It had a relative in
> Middle Dutch *pleien* 'to dance about, jump for joy',
> but this has now died out, leaving it in splendid
> but puzzling isolation, its ancestry unaccounted
> for. Its underlying meaning appears to be 'to make
> rapid movements for the purposes of recreation',
> but already in Old English times it was being used
> for 'perform on a musical instrument'.

I puzzled over this, returning again and again to these two most ancient meanings of the word, and here I describe some of this process. The diversion turned out to be quite a long one, and on the face of it has little to do with genetics or ethics. Nevertheless, it was through trying to identify the essential ingredients of playing – how we recognise it when we see it, how we distinguish playing well from playing badly – that I came to understand the connection.

Playing music

I began by looking at playing music. From very early on the verb *to play* had the dual meaning of play as the playing about of children, and as making music on an instrument. The same double meaning is present in several other languages including French, German and Russian. The double meaning does not, however, indicate that the two acts are equivalent. Ask any serious musician, and you will be left in no doubt that playing an instrument properly is not 'playing about'.

What does the proper playing of music demand of the player? Based on an extensive experience of late-night conversations with musicians, the proper playing of music usually involves fidelity to the composer's score, often as a collaborative effort with other players in an ensemble or group, and sometimes with a conductor present to provide overall leadership. (There are exceptions to all of these statements because music is art and not accountancy.)

To fulfil these requirements for doing music properly musicians need to choose the *instrument that is right* for them. The right instrument is the one that will allow the fullest expression of their musical capabilities. Simply finding the right instrument is not enough, though, and to express his or her musical capabilities a musician must eventually *learn how to play* it. This entails more than knowing the fingering to produce a D flat; it also involves becoming so familiar with the instrument's idiosyncrasies that they can be fully exploited. Paradoxically, it is only through submission to the constraints set by the nature of the instrument – the hard reality that it is a bassoon and not a xylophone – that the instrument can be rightly used. These constraints should be tested, and musicians will also acknowledge the importance of experiment, but in the end you do not make the fullest musical use of a bassoon by hitting it with a stick.

A serious musician's life revolves around *practice*, which is graft: repetitive, often tedious but (unfortunately) rarely mindless, as much a part of the fabric of life as prayer for the contemplative or eating for the rest of us. Playing also requires *listening*. This might seem self-evident, but there are plenty of music teachers who will assure you that it is not. In between player and instrument – two separate entities, subject and object – is a space in which music emerges. What happens in listening is that the player is scrupulously *attending to* this emergence.

The proper playing of music usually, but not always, involves *fidelity to the intentions of the composer*. But however closely the player or ensemble may try to follow the composer's written instructions, the ideal of absolute reproduction is unattainable and also undesirable. The creative aspect of music making is not confined to the act of composition. Each player, however faithfully she tries to stick to the score, translates the little black dots on the page in her own unique way, and has her own way of conveying this understanding through her body and out of the instrument. So fidelity contains a sense of an inevitable falling short.

All these elements – right instrument, learning to play, the disciplines of practice and listening, fidelity – can be thought of as expressions of two more general aspects. *Respect* includes the attitude to the instrument's capacities and limitations, and its material reality: you keep it dry, you wipe the rosin off the strings, you keep it tuned. The player also respects the material reality of the instrument's environment, which is why she has it insured, while the discipline of practice and the care given to the relevant parts of her body shows respect for her unique contribution to the system out of which music emerges. There is the respect given to the other players, involving the same kind of attention but multiplied by however many others are present. And ultimately all this is rooted in respect for the task at hand. If a musician loses faith in music, she might as well give up.

By this point, most of the musicians I know would be making derisive noises and pointing out how often they skip practice or grind resentfully through it, maltreat their instrument or (more likely) their bodies, or bitch about the other players or the conductor. As human beings they experience the limitations imposed by their particular physical and psychological quirks and, being human, fall short of every ideal to which they aspire. While acknowledging that this is the inevitable human reality, the important point is to see what is asked of the player *trying* to do music properly.

What develops between player and instrument is a *relationship*. (Musicians do love their instruments.) We are most used to thinking of relationships as developing between people, or at least between living things, and not between a person and an inanimate object. But if a relationship is a bond between two entities, which develops out of the interaction between them, then clearly a musician has a relationship with her instrument. It is not like the relationship she has with her partner, but equally not the same as the one she has with her toothbrush. Is she changed by the relationship? Certainly – both in the grand scheme of her life, and on the small scale of how that day's practice affects her. How does the instrument contribute to the relationship? This is much harder to answer. As an inanimate object without its own consciousness it's hard to see how it can. Nevertheless, it is apparent that handing Nigel Kennedy a school violin would result in something different from combining him with a Stradivarius. In this experiment, the player remains constant and the instrument is the variable, and the data suggest that the identity of the instrument is important to the relationship.

Music emerges within this relationship. It is not simply that the player makes the music come, though that is a large part of the story, nor that the instrument is just the source of the sound. It is the encounter between the two, in the space created by both sets of constraints, where player and instrument overlap and are more than either alone, that produces something worth hearing.

There is one other essential feature, connected to both respect and relationship. Playing music is grounded in an exacting discipline, and nobody in their right mind would voluntarily put themselves through it unless in some way it gave them pleasure. For a player, the *enjoyment* of music is a product of the relationship of respect with her instrument: obedience to the constraints of the relationship and transcendence of them.

Child's play

Up to this point I had found that thinking about the right way of playing an instrument enabled me to isolate a collection of important characteristics, broadly to do with respect and relationship. There was much that resonated with how I experienced science, whether in the epiphanies I wrote about in chapter 1 or in mundane work at the bench. Still, there was something not quite right in the parallel. It was too unidirectional. Although the nature of the instrument is important to the relationship, it doesn't contribute quite enough in comparison with the player. Seen from the perspective of a biological scientist, an instrument is not living. A saxophone can be broken but it can't be killed. And because of that, the analogy lacked the unpredictable, responsive *otherness* that for me is inherent in scientific encounter.

I want to emphasise that this limitation has more to do with the constraints of my biography than with the analogy itself. On reading early drafts of this book, my partner, a musician, took me to task for my focus on the interaction between player and instrument, and – rightly – pointed out that I was woefully neglecting the relationship between the players in an ensemble, and between players and audience. There are two reasons for this. One is that these relationships take us into another dimension of complexity, and I found it hard to move in that direction through considering music. And this in turn is due to the second, and more fundamental, reason, which is that never having played in an ensemble I lack the experience to make these relationships real for me. It is not that the analogy doesn't work (and if there are Friends reading this for whom it does work, and who can take it further, so much the better); it is that it doesn't work *for me*.

So I turned to the second of the two meanings of play I mentioned earlier. I am drawing here on the work of the psychoanalyst

Donald Winnicott and the far-reaching importance he attributed to the concept of play. Winnicott, who died in 1972, was the first British paediatrician to train as a psychoanalyst, and one of the few analysts whose writing anyone would read for enjoyment of its style. In his work with children, he found himself needing to pay a lot of attention to how they played. Moreover, he consciously used play strategies in his treatment of children (and sometimes of grown-ups as well), and went so far as to call psychotherapy a sophisticated form of play between two consenting adults. He did not, therefore, look on play simply as mucking around in a sandpit, but as a major component of people's interactions with each other at all ages.

Play serves a special function at the age when a very young child is learning to distinguish between itself (me) and the rest of the world (not-me). Coming to terms with the realisation that there is an awful lot of stuff in the environment 'out there' which is not only not-me, but is so *much* not-me that it is quite outside my control, is demanding. Winnicott suggested that a child deals with it by playing with the idea, or better by playing *in* it, using what he called transitional objects. These are the grubby, tattered, often soggy blankets or teddy bears or unlikely items of clothing on which children become fixated and from which, for a time, they cannot be parted without a struggle. To a child, its transitional object is partly me but also, more and more obviously, not-me, and in this way it forms a bridge between the inner and outer worlds.

The idea of an intermediate area of experience that does not belong exclusively to internal or external reality, but contains bits of both, is important to play. It is the place where imagination develops. When, eventually, the teddy bear loses importance and is painlessly left behind, its function as a bridge between inner and outer reality becomes spread over a much larger territory. While grasping the idea that there is a firm boundary between me and not-me is fundamental to a sense of identity, the no-man's-land where this boundary becomes fuzzier is 'the place where we live' most of the time. That is, the continual experience of the world outside is constantly woven into the 'texture of the imagination'. The phrase 'the place where *we* live' indicates not only that each one of us inhabits this space, but that it is also where we encounter everything and everyone else – not in our inner world, and not in theirs, but in the territory we make between us.

The overlapping territory between the inner and outer worlds is also where we are when we perform cultural activities like 'listening to a Beethoven symphony or making a pilgrimage to a picture gallery or reading *Troilus and Cressida* in bed, or playing tennis' (Winnicott, 1991: 105). One reason why there is a necessary connection between this hypothetical no-man's land and cultural activities is that, from the outset, what goes on here is *creative*. The very small child using a teddy to help it make an immense developmental step, is an exemplar of the human ability to make creative use of whatever is at hand to do what needs to be done. The child's act of joining up its inner world with the details of the world outside is continued by the adult trying to make sense of what's going on out there. Following the stepwise development from concrete transitional objects, to imaginative play alone, to shared playing with others as the not-meness of others is fully explored, to cultural experiences, Winnicott was led to conclude that for both child and adult, creativity only emerges when we are at play.

If that's right, then perhaps this is the key to the link I make with science. And perhaps it says something about why the analogy with playing music was ultimately inadequate. For me – and this may reflect my own limitations rather than anything more profound – playing an instrument has too much following of a given pattern, too little spontaneity, for the analogy to work. Nevertheless, before this limit is reached there may be commonalities worth looking at. Focusing on the model of play as something that goes on in this strange area between the inner and outer realities, what sorts of things are key to proper play?

Any creative activity – play or science or friendship or anything else – needs *freedom* to move around imaginatively and to make discoveries. Play of the kind I am thinking about is essentially aimless, although of course in competitive games it is turned into a ritualised expression where it does have goals (in more senses than one). But creative play remains an exploration of unknown areas where the endpoints cannot be known in advance.

To make the most of this freedom, playing has to be grounded in *trust*. It must be possible to rely on your environment and your companions being consistent and nonmalevolent. I put it like this deliberately, rather than suggesting they should simply be safe, because they may not be totally *safe* in the sense of lacking any mental or physical risk. Part of the excitement of play is precisely this edge of riskiness. But if you perceive your environment as fundamentally untrustworthy you will be unable to move around very freely, in either a physical or a psychic sense, let alone feel free to let go and play. Most of us will have encountered people (and some of us will be people) whose early world was so malevolent or unreliable as to leave them too damaged to meet others in the territory between, that is to play.

It does not contradict the need for freedom to say that play also calls for *respect*. Respect for the outside world evolves as the boundary between me and not-me becomes clearer. Not-me is recognised as separate and existing in its own right. My imagination begins to explore the components of the external world, not as outgrowths of myself but as separate things with their own properties. They are not part of me and moreover, they are not (much) under my control. The obstinacy of external reality replaces illusions of omnipotence with a healthy respect for the independent existence of the stuff 'out there'. Authentic respect

needs to grow out of the experience of having tested the constraints of the outside world: so that, for example, however hard
your parents try to prevent it, genuine respect for gravity may
require a few painful encounters with the floor.

If the external world does not come at us unmediated but is
comprehended through internal processes of interpretation and
imagination (and I don't think this is a particularly controversial
suggestion), it means that our respect for outer reality needs to
be complemented by respect for our inner world as well. In this
context respect does not mean straightforward admiration,
although I defy anyone to explore human cognition, decision
making, intuition and imagination and not be awed by them. As
with playing an instrument, respect here means exploring your
own capabilities and extending them as far as you can, so that you
know what you are able to do, and do well, when necessary. This
kind of exploration involves coming up against your limitations,
and having both the honesty and the courage to face them and
acknowledge situations where your imagination, sympathy and
ability to comprehend may be inadequate.

Where, in fact, you may need to turn to other people to supple-
ment your own abilities – which is how relationship with others
involved in the enterprise comes in. Once children start playing
together they have to develop sensitivity towards others and respect
for their needs, otherwise play collapses into conflict and there are
tears before bedtime. At the adult level, any collective endeavour –
running an office, throwing a party, meeting for worship – similarly requires a degree of sensitivity and respect for other people's
otherness. What Winnicott called the place where we live, where I
encounter other people, is creative and dynamic because what I
meet there is not-me. When we meet other people in this way we
play with a foot inside their inner worlds as well, and that is what
makes where we live a rich place and not a solitary headland.

Any one of these features – freedom, trust, respect, relationship with others – would make child's play an activity to be taken seriously. If it really is the case that playing calls for the negotiation of all of them, then doing play properly, whether as child or adult, makes formidable *disciplinary* demands. Acquiring the self-discipline to temper freedom with respect and not mutilate your teddy bear, learning the self-control to wait your turn, to share your ideas, or to listen to what others have to say and not thump them when they take your toys, are not trivial matters. This degree of discipline is difficult (so much so that quite a lot of us never manage it, at any age). But it is also non-trivial in that it is an absolute prerequisite for being able to play properly, and therefore for encountering the world and other people in any real sense.

I realise that the description I have given of child's play makes it sound like a cross between SAS training and the Ignatian exercises. If what a baby learns to do as it begins to mesh its imagination with the outside world really is the precursor to all human creative engagement, giving rise to art and music and also to science, then play is arguably one of the most valuable things we ever learn to do, and has to be taken seriously. But just as in the example of playing an instrument, it is precisely because the demands are so great that the compensation must be substantial. We're back with *enjoyment* again. Many of us may never know the enjoyment of playing music – some of us will have had lessons but remain at a loss as to why anyone would associate the experience with enjoyment – and so we may not be able to relate on a personal level to the first play-metaphor I looked at. But except for the most catastrophically damaged of people, each of us has, at some point in our lives, played, and we know experientially that play is enjoyable.

Playing science

I began by trying to follow my intuition that 'playing' scientifically is not reprehensible, but a rich part of my encounter with creation through science. There were two meanings of playing that I thought more relevant here than others. By picking a trail through each of them I began to tease out the features of playing well that were most strongly consonant with my ideas about doing science: respect, relationship and enjoyment. For me (and I emphasised how biased this judgement was) the musical analogy fell short in its ability to parallel my experience of the scientific encounter. This gave a clue to a characteristic worth particular attention. In investigation I move towards something, and the creativity of the encounter lies in the sense I make of what comes back in return, *especially* when that response cannot be entirely predicted. As a scientist, I am not *playing the world* to find out how it works or even elicit a good result, a nice tune. In scientific investigation the world and I are *playing together* 'in his presence continually.'

Scientific investigation resembles play because it happens within a relationship formed as minds try to comprehend the workings of the outside world. It may be that in their formality and rigour, the procedures of science (designing experiments, establishing controls, replicating the results) more closely resemble the structured relationship of playing an instrument, while the basic motivation behind science is closer to the desire simply to make sense of things. I would not want to be too schematic about it. Most like play, it seems to me, are the various forms of thinking that weave in between the basic motivation and the ordered procedures of scientific method: logical thought, displayed by the stereotypical scientist in a white coat, but also imaginative, intuitive, emotional, prosaic, strategic, poetic, empathic, discursive, wild. The history of science is littered with stories about discoveries made as a result of nonrational, illogical, *playful* modes of thought. In her account of the discovery of DNA, Angela Tilby considers that Watson and Crick succeeded because 'they were open to their own immaturity and foolishness. They played, they despaired, they drank wine, they built models like children.' She contrasts this with Rosalind Franklin who was held back by lacking 'the gift of play and laughter, and even a necessary streak of cruelty. Some childlike element was missing in her creativity' (Tilby, 1989: 46, 44).

I can't claim to have made any significant discoveries in genetics, but I can provide some personal experiences where scientific engagement was closer to imaginative play than anything else:

• My PhD research required me to put bits of DNA, containing genes suspected of involvement in breast cancer, into mouse or human cells growing in plastic dishes. Because it was thought that discrete genes are implicated in several changes leading, step by step, through stages of abnormality to a full-blown tumour, the idea was to insert each gene separately into the cells and see the changes it caused. This sounds a lot easier than it was. Often the gene failed to go in, sometimes it went in and nothing happened, or produced changes that could not be interpreted, and sometimes the same gene gave rise to inconsistent changes. Sometimes the cells just curled up and died.

   To understand what was going on I had to imagine what the gene, once it got into the cell, might have done to produce the results. Much more imagination than deductive ability was needed here; or rather, the imagination came first, then I thought about whether it was plausible or not. Sometimes it really was graphic imagination. I would visualise myself on the scale of the DNA and cell components, and mentally run an animated cartoon of what I thought might happen. Sometimes this was helpful, sometimes not.

• Other kinds of thinking were more intuitive. Trying to interpret results in the light of biological theory was like feeling my way at the edge of a foggy landscape, at once unfamiliar yet not exactly unknown (me and not-me again). All my most fruitful times in the lab had the flavour of making it up as I went along.

- And finally, I now think my career as a scientist came to an
  end when I started to take it all too seriously, especially the
  business of getting results. In authentic Zen fashion, when I
  didn't try hard, it worked; once I stopped playing, it didn't.

It could well be argued that all aspects of life – not just cultural
activities, and not just genetics – fit this description, and so could
be related to play. I wouldn't disagree. I would actually go further
than Winnicott, who sometimes seemed only to consider high
culture in his theory, forgetting about the everyday creativity
people display in getting on with living. But there are two particular reasons why I needed to pay attention to the connection
between play and science.

Alienation from science

The first is that, even if we can accept that cultural activities
bear some ancestral relationship to children's play, we tend not
to think of science as being 'cultural' in the way music or painting is. Perhaps it is because many of us are engaged in music or
art as amateurs (meaning, as lovers), and our direct experience
gives us an appreciation of what those professionally involved
get up to. Science is a more restricted activity, and although
some of us enjoy it vicariously through reading *New Scientist* or
watching television documentaries, there is less opportunity for
amateur involvement. Inevitably, what most people see of
science is its technological implementation, not its creative side.
And disciplines like molecular biology, again in contrast to music
or even astronomy, are less open to aesthetic appreciation. The
starry night sky is beautiful in itself; a rack of plastic tubes holds
little appeal unless you grasp the significance of what they
contain.

Science is often too alien to be seen as a cultural activity. But
most of us know what it is like to play, and thinking of science this
way gives us all a degree of access to the experience.

But what about when it all goes wrong?

The second reason I connect science and play is a practical one, and a paradox: the consequences of misusing gene technology are so great that we dare not take it all too seriously.

I know this sounds contrary. Surely it's here, when we turn a cold eye on science's moral failures, that the parallel with play must break down? If music is not played properly the worst that can happen is a cacophony, a disgruntled composer and an audience wanting their money back. The sky does not fall, the markets continue to trade, the band lives to play another day. Again, if play comes to grief in the sandpit, the consequences are individually painful but not the cause of widespread havoc.

A powerful technology, like modern genetics, is different. Some of the worries were outlined in earlier chapters. I emphasised there that, at the moment, nobody can be sure how many of these fears are well founded and which ones are most likely to happen, and so a large helping of scepticism should be employed around utopian visions and doomsday scenarios alike. But nevertheless, the predictions of genetic discrimination, creation of a genetic underclass, decreased tolerance of randomness and diversity, the uncontrolled spread of genetically modified organisms released into the environment, or possibly even the outbreak of novel or drug-resistant diseases, *could* come true. *If gene technology is not used wisely it could lead to widespread, long-term, irrevocable harm.*

The trouble is that it's a huge responsibility, and we know it. Coupled with the feeling of uncertainty in a technically complex area, the awareness can be paralysing. Time and again, I have encountered people grappling with genetic ethical issues and coming to a grinding mental halt, unable to move in any direction. From what they say, it seems that their problem is being overwhelmed by unfamiliarity, complexity, and the terrifying need to get it right. Too acute an awareness of responsibility, and the fear of the consequences of a mistake, are disempowering and leave us unable to exercise discernment. The end result can be a refusal to engage with it, or a retreat to the safety of being either all for or utterly opposed to gene technology. (The retreat to polar convictions is, I believe, the more harmful strategy. Opting out does at least leave open the possibility of future engagement; changing a fixed opinion is much harder.)

A counterbalance for the incapacitating weight of responsibility is to become more playful. Some Friends may find this suggestion irresponsible or flippant; I'm entirely serious. This chapter has shown that the true significance of play is to do with qualities like respect, trust, and relating, all of them about as far from triviality or carelessness as you can get. It should be apparent that playfulness absolutely does *not* mean jumping into whatever form of genetic manipulation comes to mind, on the grounds that it's great fun and will all come out in the wash. Sophia, playing at God's side in creation, is the personification of Wisdom. Biblical scholars interpret her variously as representing 'creation, love, life, truth, social order and wisdom' (Camp, 1995: 135), but for us she could be an allegory of the need to bring care and attention into the game. Wisdom helps to ensure the play goes well. It is also possible that to be wise, we must know how to play.

What I suggest is that too much anxiety and conscientiousness are lethal to the creativity we need here; we risk getting it grimly wrong, because we want so dearly to get it right. Think of the way young children throw themselves at questions with the same enthusiasm they bring to playing, and contrast it with the nervous silence of older children who have learned to be afraid of getting the wrong answer. Bringing a playful spirit to ethical engagement will free us to tackle new ideas without being put off by the fear of seeming stupid, and to let our hearts and imaginations roam a little more adventurously. It might then be easier to identify what we really feel most passionately about, and find constructive solutions instead of retreading the same old paths.

Playing with ideas and issues we form a relationship with them, and with other people who are engaging in the same way, out of which evolve new ways of being and believing. The next chapters move on to consider the moral meaning of relationship, and what it implies for the right ways of implementing genetic technology.

5

ETHICS IN RELATIONSHIP

What is more, the place is
not found but seeps
from our touch in
continuous creation, dark
embracing cocoon around
ourselves alone, dark
wide realm where we walk
with everyone.

Thom Gunn, Touch

In the previous chapter I mapped out the route my thinking took as I explored the connection between genetic research and ideas about play. In both analogies there seemed to be certain constraints that were prerequisites for doing play properly. For me, scientific exploration is more like child's play than playing an instrument, in that it happens as an encounter between the human mind and the workings of the outside world. For that encounter to be a good one certain rules about maintaining a relationship of respect must be observed.

Out of this encounter come observations, interpretations, hypotheses and theories, which we try to fit together into a coherent scientific framework. As new understanding is put to use, the scientific encounter generates technologies. Just as importantly, it also generates changes in thinking. Shifts in our understanding of genetics like those described in chapters 2 and 3 transform our attitudes towards human identity, the idea of human nature, responsibility and freedom, what is meant by the family, and relationships with other species. Ethical concern over gene technology tends to focus on its practical implementation, but we always need to keep in mind its less tangible impact on everyday thinking.

The idea of science as a form of play gives some insight into the ethics of scientific *research*. The rules for doing play properly may also have something to say about how genetics should be *put to use*. In terms of the motivation for doing it, research in genetics is separable from putting the results into practice as technology; for many scientists *knowing* is the key, and the utility of their knowledge is irrelevant. (This does not mean that splitting research from its consequences is generally a good thing.) This is a difficult attitude to maintain in a society where the primary rationale given for government funding of research is that science contributes to 'wealth creation', and I mourn the loss of a science that was not predicated on corporate values. But before getting too pious about the evils of commercially oriented research, a similar point can be made about giving money to medical charities in the expectation of concrete results. Few nonscientists would dip into their pockets if cancer research appeals said something closer to the truth: 'We need money to do basic research into how cells work. We find this important and fascinating, but really we can only hope that one day it will help to cure cancer.' In today's society science must have the psychological and economic pull of being useful, and other motivations seem to be illegitimate.

It is true that good technology is about being useful, and helping people and other species to flourish, and on these grounds there is a lot that is right about putting genetic research to work. But not everything about it is right, and it's in putting it to work that the acute ethical dilemmas arise, as chapter 3 noted.

Love and creativity

I have used the phrase 'relationship of respect' for what could also be described as love. It's partly because I think love (the word!) has been trivialised by being used too freely, especially in the school of religious discourse that finds it easier to talk abstractly *about* love than about showing it in practical human action. But acknowledging, respecting and valuing the otherness of whatever it is you are playing with – your bassoon or your teddy bear or other members of your own species – is to love the other in its otherness.

Many of us in the Society of Friends and elsewhere continue to hold on, however impossible and incomprehensible it may seem, to our belief that God is love. This is not just a pillar of Christian doctrine. Some of the evidence for it is provided by experience. At different times and in different places, people have reported experiencing God as love. It is not a universal claim, of course, because not everyone has the experience, or (put another way) not everyone would recognise that description. Nevertheless, it's a widespread enough account to be taken seriously. And love is experienced within relationship. For those whose encounter is a personal one, the love *of* God may be the best way to put it; those who encounter it more impersonally may prefer to talk of experiencing God *as* love, or as a context of love. The preposition used is probably of more importance to theological neatness than to the person trying to make sense of their experience. However we choose to express it, love met in relationship affirms the value of otherness as well as sameness, and the readiness to move towards the other and to risk being changed by the encounter.

For me, God seems to work in something like the following way. There is a creative and sustaining energy in the universe, which is realised in relationship with others. Our own and others' experience of God only enables us to speak for the human species, but we can believe – and many people do have this intuition – that this relationality is how God is expressed elsewhere, including through nonhuman species. It also makes sense that God's most fundamental activity is as a creator, not on the grounds that 'the creation' comes before anything else, but because creation/creativity is the process of things 'going on going on'. It is easy to slip into thinking of God's creativity as only to do with dramatic, singular events – the creation of the universe or of life on earth – especially if, as I suggested earlier, they are more conducive to mystical experience. The central theme of the first Genesis creation story, however, is that creation brings order out of chaos and continues to sustain that order against coming apart again. In this picture creation is a never-ending story, and the world's continued existence depends on God's unceasing creativity.

The care and maintenance of creation do not entail reaching a state that works and then safeguarding it against all change, nor allowing change to unfold only according to a predetermined plan. It means more that God, acting within/through physical and biological mechanisms, provides the energy that enables life to evolve in a dynamic and non-determined way. Within such freedom and indeterminacy, it seems implausible that God directly micromanages events. Twentieth-century process theology refers to God *luring* us; I don't like this formulation because it makes God sound distinctly underhand. I prefer to picture God providing indicators or attractors, moral and aesthetic magnets that we can, if we wish, use to align our actions. In traditional language this might be formulated as responding to God's call.

Because God is in relationship with what carries on being created, the creativity of God is also loving. This brings us back to the idea of love expressed as a relationship of respect of otherness. The value of each part of the creation lies in its being what it is, its identity, which includes its other-than-Godness (as well as its likeness to God).

And creativity, as the moment by moment re-creation of relationship, is mirrored in playing. Both the musical and the childish analogies called for a relationship of respect (or love). Such a relationship combined an adherence to the constraints that keep the whole enterprise from going off the rails, with a passion for playing that makes it worth doing. Seeing play as a creative *engagement* with the external world, paralleling the scientific engagement, makes visible the creativity inherent in science: not just in genetic research, but also – and this is important for its ethical evaluation – in putting gene technology to everyday use.

Moral responsibility

Ethics examine our understanding of the morally right way of doing things. There are many ways into ethics, and many recent books that consider genetic issues in the light of different ethical theories (some resources for further reading are given at the end of this book). I want to concentrate here specifically on the connection between relationship and moral responsibility, focusing on some relevant contemporary trends in ethics. This will also be relevant to the next chapter, where I consider what a Quaker bioethics might be like.

Technology increases our moral burden, both because it amplifies the *consequences* of our actions, on an individual and collective level, and because it enables us to see those consequences at work. One hundred years ago we had much less moral responsibility for polluting the atmosphere, because we were unaware of the long-term effects. Ironically, it is technology that made possible the atmospheric measurements, the computer modelling, the television programmes and other mass media that revealed the problem and brought it to our collective attention. Now that we have this knowledge, it is no longer morally responsible to focus on the immediate impacts of our decisions and leave their long-term ramifications to providence. And since we also know now that our decisions affect other world communities, present and future, and other species, our moral responsibility extends to cover them as well. To make matters worse, genetic advances seem to be taking us into areas where there are no preexisting moral guidelines. Moral responsibility of this magnitude is overwhelming, and feeling overwhelmed is rarely conducive to thinking or acting well.

It can be helpful to think of moral responsibility not as following a set of rules, nor even as an obligation to get the right answer, but as the willingness to face a problem: to perceive it, respond to it and work through it. Modern ethics ('modern' being anything after the eighteenth-century Enlightenment, in marked contrast to molecular biology where data more than five years old verge on the prehistoric) focus on *rational decision making* by the *individual*. Medical ethics were originally a professional code of conduct to prevent doctors behaving badly, and so they give the individual doctor-patient relationship a special status, almost as if it were hermetically sealed off from everyone else. Western culture has also tended to hold fairly rigidly to the idea that only autonomous and rational individuals are capable of making moral decisions. (Historically, the criteria of rationality and autonomy have been used to deny moral personhood to groups such as women, non-whites, mentally ill people, children and so on.) The focus on autonomy has neglected, and in some cases been actively hostile towards, the individual's connection with the rest of the world. Furthermore, coherent moral choices have been seen as based solely on reason: in the Cartesian separation of mind and body, rationality was associated with the civilised rather than bestial bits of human identity, and therefore with the ability to behave morally. Conventional moral philosophy has tended to shy away from the more irrational aspects of thinking, like intuition and feelings, as being irrelevant or even damaging to ethics.

Recent trends in ethics have been sceptical about whether this is an accurate representation of how people make moral decisions. Cognitive scientists have questioned the assumptions that only rationality is objective, or that it is objective at all, or that emotions simply get in the way of making good moral judgements. Emotions are being reinstated as ethicists acknowledge that feelings of shame or outrage, and the simple desire to lead a good life, are fundamental to moral orientation. Meanwhile, feminist ethics have developed alternative models, such as the ethics of care or dialogical ethics, in which the ability to act morally is not something you *possess* but something that is formed through your connections with others.

Collective ethics – examples are communitarianism, in which communities rather than individuals determine the common good, and communicative ethics, which emphasise the formation of moral opinion through dialogue – are also coming back into fashion. More important than the details of the different approaches, the revival of interest suggests that an over-individualised ethic has been found inadequate for present day purposes.

A point to note in passing, and to keep in mind for the next chapter, when we look at individual and corporate discernment in Quaker terms, is that collective ethics are not just individual ethics writ large. A collective ethic has different ways of perceiving moral issues, different ways of framing the questions and different tools at its disposal, so it should not be surprising if it comes to different conclusions. It is possible for something to be morally acceptable (although perhaps not ideal) on an individual level and morally unacceptable on a collective one. For instance, a woman or couple who are expecting a baby where there is a chance of transmitting a 'severe' (as the law puts it) genetic disorder may decide that the morally right thing to do is to have prenatal genetic diagnosis and terminate an affected pregnancy. From the viewpoint of collective ethics, however, it may be morally wrong if this private act sends out the public message that the lives of disabled people are generally not worth living.

Contemporary ethics also recognise the importance of context in providing clues to a problem. Without denying the need for generally applicable rules, individual concrete circumstances are being given greater moral weight instead of being dismissed as irrelevancies to be got out of the way before the real business starts. As an example, it is difficult to decide whether prenatal genetic testing is morally justified or not without having some particular condition or conditions in mind, and sometimes specific personal circumstances as well. (I suspect that even when considering genetic diagnosis in the abstract, somewhere in our minds there is a concrete picture, often shaped by our own history, which conditions how we think.)

A corollary of context being important is that decisions are always based on inadequate knowledge, because it is impossible to be aware of absolutely every factor relevant to a given situation. This is the 'scandal of particularity' in human terms; because we are made flesh in a particular time and place, circumstances set limits to our insight, which means having to accept that our ethical decisions will always be, at best, 'good enough' rather than perfect or even right.

An ethic that takes relationships seriously pays less attention simply to regulating the activities of participants, and more to the encounter as an intrinsically ethical process in which people work out the kind of life they find worth living and how each can best be enabled to live it. Relationships between individuals develop within family, social and political structures that profoundly affect the kinds of connections it is possible to have, or even to imagine. Taking relationships seriously can therefore counterbalance Western ethics' focus on the individual, which has tended to ignore the effect of larger social and political structures and to overemphasise personal morality (often reduced to who has sex with whom) as the sole focus of ethical concern. In contemporary bioethics, thankfully, closer attention is now being paid to the wider issues of power, and how individual choices are made within a framework of constraints that may be invisible. So, for example, we are beginning to see ethical analyses of how access to genetic information may be used to shore up particular social or economic systems and to disadvantage alternatives.

'Ordinary' ethics

There is a growing literature on specialised areas of genetic ethics, largely written by philosophers, theologians, policy makers and doctors on their days off. What strikes me is the huge gap between the theory-driven writing, and any sense that these matters are really experienced, or that experience can contribute to our moral evaluation as relevantly as scientific data or ethical theory. I first encountered this in my time as Joseph Rowntree Quaker Fellow (1995-6), when I gave workshops on genetic ethical issues to British Friends. Exploring a concrete but fictitious dilemma, it quickly became apparent that not only was context very important to the process of moral evaluation, but that the way it was used could differ markedly from a professional ethicist's. For instance, the timespan over which the dilemma was evaluated could be much longer – a lifetime, rather than the snapshot view of a medical ethical case history. The personalities of the people involved and the quality of their relationships took on a new significance as well.

Another gap between professional and what, for want of a better term, might be called 'ordinary' moral evaluation is that a professional ethicist is generally expected to stick to one major ethical theory, whether that is a theory of justice, utilitarianism, virtue theory, the appeal to rights, communitarian ethics or whatever. But working out a moral orientation is not the same thing as elaborating an ethical argument, and 'ordinary' moral competence is as much artful as it is logical. Elsewhere I have described it as moral collage (Scully, 2002). The reality of this was brought home when, some time after the Rowntree Fellowship, I was faced with making my own decision about testing for a minor genetic condition. The experience made me even more conscious than before that most people have to make medical/genetic decisions, especially prenatal ones, from a standing start and under impossible time pressures. I had the advantage of having already done some thinking on these issues, and (through the Rowntree work) having had literally hundreds of Friends do a lot of thinking for me. In this situation, whatever skills I could lay claim to *as an ethicist* were of fairly limited use. Ethical analysis did clarify some areas, but it could not help with my wildly fluctuating emotions, nor with what came to seem the primary task: not so much making a decision, as living with the decision I came to.

I think what matters most to someone devising a workable moral structure is keeping faith with his or her core values at each stage in the process. Quaker core values are things like the sacredness of every person, the importance (some of us would say sacredness) of all creation, relationship, truth-telling, acceptance of responsibility, freedom, justice, protecting the vulnerable, and valuing diversity (for more detail on this see Scully, 2002). By values, I mean the often unarticulated foundation of our moral ideal: the images, colours and flavours of the kind of life we would wish to lead. Values define the goals – the place we want to get to. Ethical principles, on the other hand, indicate the tactics we might use to get there. A principle is not a rule nor, put in theological language, a command from God. It is shorthand, a memo to ourselves about responding to our moral or religious perception. We hope that, at our best, reason and feeling are in harmony with our values so that the right decisions are made almost without thought. But we are not always at our best; and ethical principles are artificial aids for those times when we are tired or frightened or defensive, and at risk of falling short of our ideal.

Moral competence

Medical ethics, the area which has most strongly shaped the gene technology discussion, tend to distort matters by concentrating on decision making. The problem with considering ethics as being only about making decisions is that it traps us into thinking of morality as a series of yes/no options. Morality is really about perceiving, comprehending and reacting to a situation, about the choices we make in creating our moral understandings and responses. I believe many of us would find it more useful to see ethics, including genetic ethics, as the art of making useful and communicable moral evaluations, rather than learning the right principle to apply in any given situation, or drawing up regulatory frameworks. Both of these are important, but not much help in fostering real moral competence.

Looking at it like this puts the emphasis on process instead of conclusion. Because traditional approaches to ethical appraisal have concentrated on rational analysis, we are relatively inept at perceiving and describing our situations in moral, ethical or indeed spiritual terms. But moral perception and imagination are as much a part of moral competence as analysis, and all of them are skills that can be developed. Furthermore, the skills of moral evaluation are just as applicable to unfamiliar areas like gene technology as they are to more familiar things, such as wars. It is particularly important that the 'genetic' component of genetic ethics, the fact that it is about science, should not become an excuse for ducking our responsibilities. (It may be much more comforting to declare ourselves scientifically illiterate than admit to being morally adrift.)

No one should be under the illusion that a general improvement in moral competence will make navigating to a stance or decision on a genetic issue any easier. Firm principles, hard rules, and moral or religious laws are attractive precisely because they offer apparent certainty, and promise to stop us getting it all horribly wrong; they also (another great attraction) minimise the degree of personal effort required. But I think that if we come to stances and decisions through genuine engagement with an issue, they will be more thoroughly worked out, spiritually grounded, sensitive, and just, than otherwise. Collective engagement must also, somewhere along the way, take into account our diversity of moral perceptions, and is more likely to generate solutions that different sides can 'live with' even if they are not in total agreement.

Relationships and moral balance

In the preceding chapter I suggested that science could be a playful encounter, and all the experiences I wrote about in chapter 1 could be described as spiritual encounters. Despite the generality of this, the kind of moral relationship that exists between those who encounter each other is not always the same. Playing can be seen alternatively as creating a relationship between subject and object, or between two subjects. In the Jewish theologian Martin Buber's writing, these two categories are carefully distinguished. The I-you relationship between two subjects is an experience of the I-Thou relationship between a human being and God. Unlike subject-object (I-it) relationships, it is participatory and it anticipates a response. In Buber's scheme, I-it relationships are not in themselves wrong, and they are often necessary for objective analysis, for management or control. But Buber felt moral wrong was done when this way of relating to another became dominant or was used inappropriately. He was particularly concerned with developing awareness of the *choice* of attitude: that whatever we encounter can be part of an I-you relationship, if we choose to see it that way.

Another Jewish thinker, Emanuel Levinas, focused on a slightly different feature of the relationship between persons, that moral responsibility must exist without any demand for reciprocation. For him, moral commitment happens when a person responds to what he called 'the Face', the simple existence of another, prior to knowing anything about them. Unlike Buber's I-you relationship, which seems to anticipate some kind of dialogue, Levinas' moral relationships expect no response – and certainly not an equivalent response – from the other. In fact, you commit to 'being for' the other without knowing whether they are or ever will be in a position to reciprocate. In Levinas' ethics, 'I scratch your back if you scratch mine' is not a moral statement.

Both of these reflections on the moral character of relationships can be useful in looking at the scientific encounter. Buber makes us think about the attitude we bring to the task: are we treating the other participants as objects, subjects, or (as might be appropriate) something in between? Meanwhile, Levinas reminds us that we make a moral commitment to the other irrespective of their responsibility for us. This is particularly relevant for the ethics of gene technology, where the people affected might be poor, vulnerable, geographically distant, or only exist in the future; they can never reciprocate, or call us to account for what we do to them.

In genetic investigation

'Right scientific *investigation*' therefore requires the right sort of relationship with whatever is being investigated. Above all else, this is a relationship of encounter, not of domination. I have a glimpse of the difference from my own research experience. In the previous chapter I described my PhD research into cancer-causing genes. In order to get a gene of particular interest into the cells, I had to construct what is called a retroviral vector. This was a cobbled-together virus that contained the gene and would infect the cells. Designing the virus was straightforward enough, but actually making it took me a year and a half (I had never been much good at handiwork, and it showed). It was vitally important, because the vector was essential for all the other experiments I planned to do. I remember vividly the night I realised I had finally done it. I happened to be on duty at a student advice centre, and took the day's results along with me. Fuelled on instant coffee and Bourbon creams, I checked and re-checked the sizes of DNA fragments, visible as smudgy fluorescent bands on black and white Polaroids. The sensation when I convinced myself that the bands had *exactly* the sizes predicted if the vector structure was correct, is indescribable. But the most important point is that, for me, the feeling had nothing to do with power-over, or my mastery of the genetic material. It was much more like a *meeting* with a long-awaited friend. I remember that I looked at the picture of my virus and said, 'Hello gorgeous.'

In gene technology

In *implementing* gene technology we are clearly enmeshed in the interactions between subjects. Putting genetics into practice establishes and affects relationships, not with a subject of study but with the people and other species affected by the way the science is used. And these relationships are diverse and often very fraught. They include relationships with *individuals*, for example in decisions about genetic diagnosis, perhaps with people who are sick or disabled or who are suffering in other ways because of genetic disorders. In these situations we are not relating to a genome but to another being, who embodies its own lived history of experiences. Then there is the network of structural relationships between *institutions* involved in gene technology, the universities and research councils, pharmaceutical and agrochemical companies, the government and other regulatory bodies, and with the political and economic systems they represent. There is our relationship with the *other animal or plant species* manipulated for our own ends, and also with the species that may be affected by the introduction of a genetically modified organism into the ecosystem. Finally there is our relationship with the *DNA* we are manipulating, and with our *ideas* about DNA.

One of the important things the play analogies brought out for me was the link between good relationships and respect. In the instrumental analogy, the musician shows respect for the capacities and constraints of the instrument and of their own skill, for the tension between discipline and freedom, for the score, and for the other players. Child's play included respect for the outer reality as well as one's own, and for the inner worlds – that is, the 'otherness' – of those with whom we play. Respect supplies the solid ground for authentic relation, and is visible in genuine acceptance of their otherness. Otherness makes a relationship real and particular, but also demands the effort of moving towards the other, and to do so our respect for them has to be engaged. What I draw from this is that love means recognising the needs and desires of both sides, and that one of the rules of playing is that both pulls must be negotiated. In the implementation of gene technology this means balancing – somehow! – our own reality, desires and goals, with those of the other as far as they can be apprehended.

This has important implications for the way we make moral evaluations in genetics. A model of ethical evaluation that takes a relationship of respect as its starting point, trying to find a balance between all sides' desires and needs, is very different from a model that pits the rights of one against the other. I have avoided so far using the language of rights in the discussion of genetic ethics. While rights are absolutely indispensable as *political* tools, they are often not very helpful *ethically*. In practice, the phrase 'a right to' can effectively short-circuit any further ethical thought. Furthermore the language of rights is often inadequate for considering beings with powers and abilities that do not fit the conventional model – embryos, for example, or cognitively impaired people, or animals. It's quite hard to think of a fruitfly as having rights, but I *can* conceive of having a relationship of respect with a fruitfly. As relationships go it may be a tad one-sided – the fruitfly is probably oblivious of me, because I am not a plum – but it still provides a context within which I can demonstrate my respect, and work out the obligations that such a relationship puts on me.

The point where we balance the moral responsibilities to ourselves and to the other, where our behaviour shows appropriate respect for both parties and for the connection between them, will depend on what is in relationship with what. Nevertheless, the simple fact that a relationship exists at all means the balance point cannot be entirely to one side. The moment we acknowledge a connection with something else, we give up the freedom to make moral choices based solely on our own desires – to do that would be a failure to respect the other. But equally – and I think this may be particularly difficult for nice, sensitive, non-exploitative, conflict-avoiding people like Quakers to bear in mind – a viable morality cannot be based exclusively on the desires of the other (or what we imagine those desires might be). Doing so effectively denies the reality that there is a bond between *both* of us. I don't mean that self-denying or self-sacrificial decisions should never be made, only that everyday morality has less to do with sainthood than with liveable compromises and with making the best shot we can at our ideals.

The point of ethical balance will shift even within the same relationship, let's say between the human doing the genetic manipulation and the mouse being manipulated, as the context changes. For example, context might include how serious the reason for the genetic manipulation of the mouse is, how likely it is to contribute to human flourishing, what impact it will have on other species, and how many mice in total will need to be used.

These insights may be particularly useful to the gene technology debate, where people tend to adopt starkly opposing positions. One person may come down firmly on the side of human priorities taking precedence, the other that it is absolutely illegitimate to manipulate the genomes of other species. One side may want genetic research to be pursued at all costs because it will produce cures for diseases or otherwise 'improve' human embodiment, while the other argues that genetic research carries too great a risk of being misused for eugenics and should therefore

be abandoned. The reminder that a moral balance based on relationship *must* carry something of both sides is a useful corrective
against adopting fixed and absolute moral standpoints. Even for
Quakers, it can be hard to relinquish the need to be completely in
the right (and sometimes the converse, a self-flagellating need to
be in the wrong).

Love in ethical evaluation

When John Woolman set out in 1763 to 'spend some time with
the Indians', he had no conventional moral guidelines for his
journey. He knew only that 'Love was the first motion', calling him
to meet otherness on its own terms.

The relationship of respect (love, in other words) can be both
starting point and beacon for ethical navigation. At each step
along the way – and especially when paths diverge and choices
are inevitable – the question is, what does this do to my relationship of respect with those others concerned? Using relationship
in this way testifies to the existence of that of God *between* us,
which enables us to connect at all. It is not (just) that in order to
be morally correct our behaviour should express this relationship,
but also that the existence of the relationship will guide the behaviour. As an ideal, we would find ourselves instinctively doing the
right thing. This model sees ethical behaviour as a series of acts
of relationship, which are necessarily aligned with the good if the
relationships are loving ones: as the poet Theodore Roethke
noted, 'Loving, I use the air/Most lovingly'. It also lives out the
trust that we will head in the right direction if we are open and
faithful enough.

I said it is an ideal and as such it is wildly idealistic, because
we are human and subject to moral myopia, tiredness and bad
temper. None of us is John Woolman, and he only put himself at risk.
When human reality is combined with the limitations imposed by
circumstances, the prospects of getting gene technology ethically

right become much less rosy. It would be wantonly naive to think that if love is our guide, or, as Friends might put it, if we act and speak in love, all else will follow. Love can run out of control, some love is pathological, and our loving commitment to one person can lead us to misuse others, or other species (which might happen in genetic medicine, for example). So the kind of relationship of respect that is relevant to moral evaluation has little to do with either overwhelming passion or vague feelings of benevolence towards all things. It's hard and conscientious work, listening to what the relationship is telling us, actively seeking out the opportunity to be guided, and being ready to re-align ourselves with the good (for the pessimists among us, the least bad) when it becomes clear we've gone astray. Essential to this is a collective as well as individual process of discernment. The next chapter looks at how this could be done in a Quaker context.

6

A QUAKER APPROACH

This shaking keeps me steady. I should know.
What falls away is always. And is near.
I wake to sleep, and take my waking slow.
I learn by going where I have to go.
Theodore Roethke, The Waking

There is no such thing as a solitary polar explorer,
fine as the conception is.
Annie Dillard, An Expedition to the Pole

What might a Quaker approach to ethics in genetic manipulation be like?

One starting point would be to consider each of the testimonies in turn to see what light they throw on ethical ways of conducting genetic research and implementing the results. Unfortunately such methodological neatness is thwarted by the way that every testimony, in the end, has something to say about every issue. It is difficult to discuss the implications for genetic testing and screening of our commitment to equality, for example, without also talking about justice, community, truth and integrity. Conversely, not everything Friends might want to say about gene technology is best presented as a testimony.

The alternative of focusing on specific genetic issues in turn and then reflecting on them as Quakers has the disadvantage of becoming repetitive. And as I have said, the hot issues of today are likely to be outdated in a few years' time – a fate I hope the testimonies won't share.

Instead, I will simply pick up a few central themes of relevance to Quaker faith and practice which have emerged in writing this book. Most of these themes will be familiar to Friends; the final one might not be, and I offer it as something new to carry into our future discussions on genetics, and science in general. Along the way I will also make some suggestions for things Friends can do *now*. These suggestions are not an exhaustive list, and I hope our exploration will go further.

That of God...

> ...be patterns, be examples, in all countries,
> places, islands, nations, wherever you come; that
> your carriage and life may preach among all sorts
> of people, and to them. Then you will come to
> walk cheerfully over the world, answering that of
> God in everyone...
>
> *(George Fox, 1656)*

The phrase 'that of God in everyone' is a cornerstone of present-day Quakerism, despite vigorous debate about its contemporary theological interpretation and how far that differs from what Fox intended to say. We use it to convey the belief that God, and our response to God, are part of human identity. People are holy ground and open to an unmediated encounter with the Light within. Other religious traditions are more likely to turn to words like 'soul' to express a similar sort of thing; the overlap is not perfect but there is workable common meaning. For European Quakers today, 'that of God in everyone' has become a claim about a fundamental human characteristic, supporting our other statements about equality, nonviolence, truth-telling and so on. Furthermore, the phrase does double-duty: while acknowledging that people have this quality in common, at the same time it recognises the validity of their differences as well.

In the genetic context it is particularly relevant to the issue of the *commodification* of people or of 'life itself'. As Quakers we have a history of witness against human commercial exploitation, most famously in our opposition to slavery. More recently many Friends have been critical of the economic ideology that sees everything – natural, human or genetic resources – as a commodity, an object with a market value, which can be bought and sold. Commodification of people is most visible when it comes in overt forms like slavery or sex tourism, but is present whenever human (and other) beings are treated as nothing more than objects of commercial value.

The question is whether genetic technologies will exacerbate this trend. When an agrochemical company manipulates and then patents genes from plants originating in the developing world, it seems to many people that this is taking commodification onto a completely new level. To what extent is 'life itself' here being exploited for profit? Or when prenatal genetic diagnosis is used to select against diseases and disabilities, are we treating people as products whose value depends on the efficiency of their 'design' rather than on their being human?

We might have opinions here but none of us knows the answers, and we ought to be immediately suspicious of anyone who claims that they do. Questions like these tend not to have straightforward answers anyway. What we should not do, however, is let that deter us from trying to clarify and respond to the issue. It may help to reflect on precedent: remember that the Quaker opposition to slavery, which seems so obvious in retrospect, began in a similar state of uncertainty. There were some Friends who saw clearly that slavery was wrong, others who were equally convinced it was not, and a larger number who needed time to work out what they thought and turn it into a corporate concern. It should be encouraging to see a historical continuity here, not just with our longstanding concern over commodification, but with our willingness to move forward by struggling with a complex issue in the Light, rather than waiting to have all the answers before we start work.

A testimony to creation?

As creator, God brings order out of chaos – order being the physical and chemical stability needed for anything to exist at all. But unchanging stability is dead, as Sylvia Plath, a poet who understood a thing or two about instability and creation, knew when she wrote that 'Perfection is terrible, it cannot have children'. Life is a *dynamic* flux, combining change with stability. A good example of this is DNA replication. When one cell splits into two, the DNA of the original is duplicated to provide a copy for the daughter cell. The enzyme machinery that does this must be accurate; it makes mistakes just often enough to introduce the occasional novelties, or mutations, which are the raw material for natural selection. In Lewis Thomas' memorable description, DNA copying manages 'to blunder slightly' at a rate that ensures both continuity and evolutionary change (Thomas, 1974).

When we talk about 'the creation' as if it were perfect and unchanging, we forget that instability is necessary, and we lose sight of God active and present in it. And when that happens, it becomes easier to think of the natural world – if not other people – as being there simply as a commodity for our use.

If creation is an activity and not an act, it cannot be quite *there* yet. (Wherever *there* is.) And if we assume for the moment that our presence here has some meaning, then where we are now – in terms of our technological as well as our moral capacities – is not accidental. We have the capacities we do because we're supposed to use them, but also (and this is very important) because we're supposed to work out the right way of using them. If God has some project in mind then in everything we do, we have the option of being God's collaborators in furthering the project rather than simply maintaining what currently exists. This holds not just for what Quakers have traditionally thought of as our collaborative work with God, conflict resolution for example. It is also true of these new tools of gene technology.

This is a key point for us, and it is important that it is not misunderstood. I *do not* mean that we are under divine mandate to create whatever novel forms of life take our fancy. Paradoxically, we can only act as responsible collaborators in the processes of creation if we have trust in it, if we have a sense of the sacrality of things as they are as well as what we could make of them. Genetic research, with its story of the extraordinary unity in diversity of living things, has the potential to enhance this awareness – which is one good reason for doing it. I *do* mean that genetic inquiry and gene technology can be used for the good of all creation, by promoting global health (not just in the rich West, which can afford sophisticated healthcare), helping to feed the hungry, and transforming how we think about other human beings and our genetic cousins with whom we share the planet. And Quakers need to involve themselves in all aspects of the practice, regulation and policy of gene technology if this goal is to be achieved.

Recent Quaker work towards a testimony to the earth, or creation, has dealt mainly with 'conventional' technologies that pollute or consume irreplaceable earthly resources, and has concentrated on minimising our environmental impact: recycling materials, reducing our use of energy, and so on. But a comprehensive testimony to the earth must also have something to say about genetic manipulation, because the ability to analyse and alter genomes places our relationship with creation in a different framework.

It will be crucial for any such testimony to keep its feet on the ground. Creation spirituality speaks to many people's desire for a religious awareness that incorporates nature and the body, and this is right and necessary. I worry, though, that some versions of creation spirituality (by no means all) make use of a very selective picture of nature. For example, they imply that everything would be all right if only humankind would stop interfering with a harmonious and balanced natural order. The data provided by the natural sciences suggest that far from being balanced, nature is constantly shifting and correcting itself (blundering slightly, if you like), and the corrections can be as drastic as collapses of the earth's crust or the extinction of a species. Meanwhile, we know from our own observation that the natural order is as full of struggle and suffering as it is of nice sunsets.

These data from science and our own experience mean we need clearer thinking about the belief that everything natural is good, or that if life is considered sacred then living things are perfect just as they are. I'm not suggesting that either of these beliefs is wrong, only that more reflection is needed, particularly on how to translate metaphysics into the everyday practice of medicine or agriculture. The painful, catastrophic, unbalanced face of nature needs to be included in our testimony. If not, the result will be to increase the split between people and nature as we become less able to comprehend the total reality of creation: its unpleasantness, as well as its beauty. It takes us back to relationship again, and the problem that Levinas identified of baulking at *otherness*, the literally *in*comprehensible parts of nature, trying to force it into a shape that fits more comfortably with our own preconceptions.

Our testimony to creation will also need to take into account the dialectical relationship between nature and the world of technology. These two meet and interact, changing each other to produce an end result different from what either would be if left to their own devices. Moreover, the combination of the natural and technologised worlds is never static, so that every 'end' is already a step towards something else. This makes things difficult, in that maintaining an ethically correct relationship between nature and technology demands our unflagging attention (we can never afford to rest on our laurels), but it is also reason to hope that the present state is always, through grace and work, redeemable.

Power and peace

Perhaps the most difficult feature of gene technology is its moral ambiguity. In an age of global interconnection and commerce, it offers some people more opportunity while simultaneously oppressing and exploiting other people elsewhere. Which people get the genetic goods is not an inevitable outcome of natural processes, but determined by prior economic and political decisions about how entitlement is distributed. Such choices are unavoidably ethical ones. They are also spiritual, because they grow out of a set of beliefs about who matters, and why.

Every technological development is taken up enthusiastically by those in power to reinforce their own position. Gene technology is no exception. 'Those in power' used to mean the national state, although increasingly the role is being taken on by transnational institutions and corporations. But it also refers to the power differentials of everyday life, which may be harder to recognise. Depending on context we might be talking about the power of employers over employees, men over women, ablebodied over disabled people, white over black, affluent over poorer, straight over gay, or human over nonhuman species. For each of these, there are already examples of genetics being coopted by one group to reinforce its superiority over the other. Thus racist beliefs have claimed support from 'proof' of the genetically determined superiority of whites; prenatal testing has been used to select against girl children; and there are forms of genetic medicine that are, or will be, available only to the relatively rich. As genetic information becomes commonplace, it could only too easily become a commonplace tool of oppression.

Power differentials have a tendency to create polarised groups unable, or unwilling, to talk to each other. 'Speaking truth to power' can be interpreted to include facilitating genuine dialogue between weaker and more powerful groups, hoping to support the voice of the weaker parties and shift both participants' horizons of understanding. Quakers, with our tradition of mediation, and the advantage of our internal diversity of opinion, may be particularly good at helping opposing agents – agrochemical companies versus green activists, say, or patent lawyers versus activists for indigenous peoples' rights, or insurers versus those with genetic abnormalities – to talk with and hear each other. We are familiar with the idea that where one group has substantially more clout than another, providing a space where both groups can speak on *equal* terms is an act of radical advocacy. It would be appropriate for Friends *now* to undertake concrete actions that enable groups in stand-off, or socially marginalised groups, to communicate on genetic issues. This would be firmly within our tradition of fostering peace and responding to the call of the most vulnerable for justice. The current moral ambiguity of gene technology makes it particularly important that both mediation and advocacy are involved. They are different skills, and on genetic issues some of us, perhaps because of a stronger personal conviction, will be drawn to the more partisan approach. One form of work need not exclude the other, nor be considered better or more Quakerly.

Truth and knowledge

One very good reason for feeling unprepared for the ethical debate about gene technology is that in reality, we *are* unprepared. As a society we don't yet know much about either the technology or its moral and social effects. Obviously we can (and do) make educated guesses and a few wild suppositions, but we have almost no experience on which to base our predictions, and not enough perspective to grasp the full implications – good, bad and banal – of the experience we do have. Part of our responsibility *now* is therefore to gather information, to work at increasing our own and society's understanding, rigorously stripping away our prejudices and mistaken beliefs so that there can be more clarity.

It's important to become as competent in these areas as possible: incompetence can be as damaging as wickedness, and is a lot more common. Becoming competent does not, however, mean acquiring expertise in molecular genetics before being able to comment on the ethics of gene technology. I have tried to show throughout this book that experts have skills that make vital contributions to moral evaluation, but simply having those skills does not mean they know the right thing to do. While a scientist may be able to sequence your DNA and an ethicist reconstruct what Aristotle would have said about it, they are not necessarily any better at discerning and acting on the good than anyone else. Developing our moral competence means becoming more adept at perceiving, describing, analysing and evaluating the truth of situations, using all the resources at our disposal. These resources include scientific ones, and so where we make use of scientific facts it is *ethically* important to be scrupulous about their accuracy and the reliability of our sources.

At the same time we need to distinguish between facts and evaluation. Although evaluations are predominantly subjective, they can be brought to their knees by a shaky factual basis. Thus, I became a Quaker for reasons that are neither correct nor incorrect, but to do with my evaluation of how Quakerism could help me lead the kind of life I aspired to. But if I told you that before founding the Society of Friends George Fox was known throughout England for his talent as a country and western singer, you would be justified in pointing out that this is *factually* incorrect. And this in turn might make you suspect that my *evaluation* of Quakerism is equally unreliable. To make convincing moral evaluations, we do therefore have a responsibility to get our facts right *and* to subject our evaluation to rigorous scrutiny, both of which require us to remain open to new light.

When incorporating new light in the form of genetic information, however, it is important not to fall into the trap of thinking that genetics can provide straightforward moral justifications.

This temptation is particularly seductive when genetic data appear to provide authority for our more benevolent intuitions about human morality. So, for example, we might find ourselves wanting to say that our genetic relatedness *is* a ground for treating all people as equals. A version of this was popular in the late 1980s, when a putative 'gay gene' was identified. Some people welcomed this as proof that homosexuality is not to be condemned, because it is genetic. At least one scientist made use of the supposed gay gene in counselling parents who were having difficulty coming to terms with their children's sexuality, telling them that because homosexuality is a normal genetic variant they could 'go back to loving their homosexual sons unconditionally'. (Gorski, 1996: 32). This sounds admirable: but consider what it says about us, if our criterion for knowing whether to love someone is not the presence of God within them, nor even the way they live, but the precise composition of a chemical extracted from their cells. As Quakers (actually, as human beings) we should be saying unequivocally that while genes 'for' sexual orientation, or any other human characteristic, tell us something fascinating about how God puts diversity into creation, they say nothing at all about the value of people – straight, gay or any point in between. The source of human significance lies elsewhere.

If incorporating new genetic information into our spiritual worldview, and working out the right way to use it, is going to take such effort then wouldn't it be easier simply not to know? As our understanding of genetics unfolds, the question of whether there are real limits to knowledge becomes increasingly salient. Just as I have tried to distinguish (fuzzily, and accepting a degree of overlap) between scientific research and its implementation in technology, I would want to draw a line here between acquiring knowledge and doing things with it. It's another fuzzy line and even harder to negotiate in practice. But although my head is aware of the potential for using genetic knowledge wrongly, my heart is convinced that knowledge, and knowing the truth, are virtues, and that human beings are intelligent, curious and tool-using because God likes us that way. Being intelligent and curious inevitably leads to dissatisfaction with the limits of what we know. I would put it as strongly as that wanting to know more, *just for the sake of knowing more*, is an act of adoration. As Sara Maitland writes, 'The more we know about what is there and how it works, the more we can perhaps know about God' (Maitland, 1995: 14), even when we discover unpalatable truths about nature or ourselves, and even when making sense of our knowledge is a struggle. Loving God in creation has some similarity to loving another human being, including the risk of finding out things about the other that are hard to cope with. And a love that steers clear of this is one that prefers safety to truth.

Transformation

Gene technology would not be controversial if the thought of using it wasn't very attractive. It holds a powerful appeal (and I think this applies even to those people who ultimately reject it) because it offers us the hope of transformation. Humans want so much to be better. The dream of being different pushes us to create things, go on quests or go to the gym, practise religion or psychoanalysis, and have ethics. It also makes us chronically dissatisfied and impatient with our rate of change. If we truly want to be different, why should it be so hard, or take so long?

Genetic manipulation seems to offer a novel and effective route to changing ourselves and our world. At heart, therefore, the attraction of gene technology is a religious one. And, as with religious transformation, we are deeply ambivalent about it: wanting to be different, but afraid of the process of dis-integration that has to be gone through, and of what life might be like afterwards.

Every newspaper article and television feature about the

'genetic revolution' predicts that it will transform our lives unimaginably in the coming years. When all around you are repeating the same story, I think it's generally a good idea to ask whether it is actually true. In this case the answer is that we don't yet know, and that it would be rash to make predictions. There will certainly be changes and innovations, but it is less clear whether they will amount to radical social and biological transformation, or whether it will be business as usual with some extra medical tests thrown in. It's fascinating that society seems to have a collective amnesia about all the other scientific and technological innovations, like the isolation of hormones or the development of nuclear power, which in their time were going to revolutionise our lives. Among the lessons of the history of technology are that the genuinely revolutionary innovations may be the least glamorous ones (it was the discovery of restriction enzymes, previously of interest only to bacteria, that opened the door to genetic technology); and that the important social effects are largely unpredictable and often indirect (nuclear power did far more damage through its distortion of civil government and the creation of a domestic 'climate of suspicion' than it did to our genomes, although it was the latter that people protested about).

Questions in science tend to take the form, 'How does that happen?', while in theology the question is more likely to be, 'Why does that happen?'. But when children play make-believe together and when artists create, they ask, 'What if...?' *What if I were a cowboy? What if I could fly?* And as children and artists get older, *What if it didn't hurt so much? What if I could remember more? What if it wasn't lost for ever? What if we could solve this some other way?* By asking the question *what if* I send my imagination somewhere it has never been, and it's impossible to return unchanged.

It may be that the most revolutionary consequence of the genetic revolution will not be the production of pig/human hybrids or a society full of clones, but the transformation that results from grappling with new ideas and crossing uncharted ethical territory. Some of this has already happened. Since assisted reproductive technologies introduced such things as surrogate mothers and egg donors, we have had to think harder than before about what a mother is, and our answers have multiplied the ways we imagine motherhood and the nature of mothers. Until recently, we have been able to leave unexamined most of our knee-jerk reactions about what a 'normal' human being is; now that prenatal genetic diagnosis is already here, and gene therapy and genetic enhancement may come, we have to examine how credible and just our criteria for normality are. It's not that these issues didn't exist before (there was always the 'problem' of the adoptive mother, for example), but more that there was no real need for most of us to bother about them. Things have changed.

This brings us back to the sense of not being morally up to dealing with gene technology. It may well be that our technological skills are outstripping our moral capacities. But it is pointless to say, 'We don't yet have the moral skill to use gene technology wisely, so we'd better not have anything to do with it.' No skill, whether it is swimming or singing or moral competence, develops without actually doing it. (Although it's wise to remember that skills are learnt gradually, and if you rush headlong into the water you can drown.)

The willingness to engage with these opportunities and problems, in the world as it is and with faith that the world could be different, inevitably pulls us towards a personal and collective transformation. Trusting that we can engage with these issues, that it is possible and even valuable to do so, is also an act of witness to the relationship we believe exists between God and ourselves.

Discernment

Western (and increasingly global) society generally favours the robust view that if something can be done, then it should be. In discussions with Friends about the new genetics, I have been struck by the pervading sense that using gene technology is inevitable and its consequences – whether good or bad – are outside our control. This needs to be challenged. As ethicists we can say that not everything that is possible is right, and as a religious group we know that not everything is *of* God, even if (some of us believe) all things are *in* God.

The theologian Jacques Ellul had a generally bleak view of technology, but he wrote positively about the 'inventiveness' needed to negotiate between the ethics of a technologically based society, characterised as a 'refusal to interfere in any way with efficiency' (Ellul, 1964: 133), and the Gospel ethics of anarchic compassion. Imagination and inventiveness will be needed to identify ways of using gene technology that are consistent with what we hold to be true as individuals and as Friends. Deciding what we should do with our technological tools requires discernment. Do Quakers have anything special to offer here?

It is possible that our history of marginalisation and our present lack of dominance within church structures are advantages for discernment. Liminal people whose values lie a bit oblique to the mainstream make their evaluations from a different perspective. They may therefore be able to discern things that others cannot. The Quaker refusal to split life into sacred and profane compartments is one example of an alternative point of view. It tells us pointedly that day to day bioethical issues are spiritual ones too. Our conviction that there is holy significance in everything may also help us see, and remind others, that bioethics are not just about the big issues of cloning or genetic enhancement. It's in the trivia of visits to the doctor and shopping for food, paying for drugs and the daily coming to terms with life in a fragile and limited body, that we most faithfully show our religious and ethical commitment.

Discernment is often much easier to practise than describe! The hints and nudges that constitute 'leading' come from a diversity of sources according to chance and taste, from rational debate to the shafts of insight I wrote about earlier. Most Quakers would agree that holding an issue in the Light is an essential part of discernment, and I won't attempt to prescribe how individuals should do that. I do want to say a bit more about the distinctive Quaker practice of *corporate discernment*.

Because the conclusions we come to may challenge society's orthodoxy (as well as surprise ourselves), they need to be well thought through and have collective support. The various forms in which Quakers exercise corporate discernment all offer ways of bringing multiple minds and hearts to bear on an issue. They cannot guarantee that the answers will be right, but they certainly raise the chances of being guided by the Spirit. Despite this, it is interesting how contemporary British Quakers draw strict lines around what is open to this exercise and what is not. We exhibit a marked reluctance to submit individual decisions to corporate discernment, especially in areas – like medicine – not traditionally recognised as spiritual. In part this reflects the strong individualism of the wider society, and a weaker sense of the discipline of the Meeting as a key feature of Quaker life. Our reluctance might also contain our anxiety about possible disagreement with other Friends. Finally, personal opinions and decisions to do with genetics are seen as private; the last thing one would want to open to public discussion.

It may be that one of our hardest tasks *now* is to challenge this, within both the Society and the wider world. Coincidentally (or perhaps not) genetics provides a potentially useful analogy. Our current reading of the relationship between genes, the individual and the community, is ambiguous. As we saw in chapter 3, the confidentiality of genetic information is a major issue in genetic ethics. The *practical* concern is that unrestricted access to other people's genetic information will lead to abuses, while the *emotional* response to this possibility is driven by the feeling that genetic information about ourselves is the most intimate of all. At the same time, our growing understanding of the genetic relatedness of human populations (and of humans with other species) has blurred the lines drawn around individuals, families and social groups, which previously seemed clear-cut. It forces us to question how we balance individual and collective rights and responsibilities. Is it possible for Friends to relate this to a changing concept of the balance between individual and corporate religious life?

If faced, say, with genetic diagnosis – which might involve very hard issues about termination of a pregnancy or the effect of a diagnosis on the rest of our lives and our families' lives – could we imagine bringing it in an appropriate way to our Meeting, perhaps to a Meeting for Clearness? Looking back on the time when I was pondering my own genetic testing, I notice that the thought never occurred to me. I was afraid of upsetting or boring people, of being misunderstood, of having 'my' problem taken over by others, and of having some settled opinions questioned (that fear of change again). But it now seems to me there was a discrepancy between my professed belief in Quaker corporate life, and my actual ability to let it anywhere near me. Do we deny ourselves the opportunity of corporate Light being cast on decisions we have to make, or opinions we have to form, because the issues don't come conveniently labelled as spiritual ones?

There are distinctions to be maintained, of course. Britain Yearly Meeting in session producing a Minute on genetic discrimination is not the same thing as my decision about genetic testing. Even on a personal level it's not an either-or choice between isolated decisions versus an orgy of gratuitous sharing, but a movement back and forth which allows individual and corporate discernment to inform each other. A personal concern about gene therapy, for example, should remain an individual's opinion, but from time to time could be exposed to collective Light. As well as helping individual discernment, it would also be a way of communicating our thoughts, fears, concerns and understanding amongst us. As Quakers, we have processes and structures for doing this and we could be making better use of them.

But opening ourselves up to the Light, particularly as a corporate exercise, requires faith. Faith is not about managing to believe improbable doctrines or toeing a theological party line, but about trusting enough to use all the intellectual, emotional and spiritual resources at our disposal to discern God's leadings and respond to them – in this case by making creative moral decisions. This is both frightening and hard work. So why do we bother? My answer to this question brings us, finally, to something not often associated with Quakerdom: enjoyment.

Enjoyment

> The moon leans down to look; the tilting fish
> In the rare river writhe, and laugh; we lavish
> Blessings right and left and cry
> Hello, and then hello again in deaf
> Churchyard ears until the starlit stiff
> Graves all carol in reply.
>> Sylvia Plath, *Love is a Parallax*

enjoy, vb (tr.). 1. To receive pleasure from; to take joy in.

It would be wrong to say that Quakers don't enjoy themselves, but as a group we often don't give the impression of 'walking cheerfully' (even if Fox didn't mean with fixed grins on our faces). It is not that we are overtly gloomy – we don't preach sin and damnation, and we have our moments of quiet humour – but on the whole Quakers are an earnest people. Authority is given to gravity (as in weighty Friends) rather than lightheartedness, which is strange considering where we believe the Light should be. Reading

Quaker literature I am struck by how seriously we take our practical witness in our testimonies to peace with justice, equality, simplicity and community. I find it humbling and moving, and it's one of the reasons I found my way to the Society in the first place. But it often leaves me with no sense of *why* Quakers work for peace, justice or equality; what it is, other than gritted-teeth duty, that motivates us.

I think we do it because we enjoy it, but we don't often say so because deep down we suspect that's an unworthy reason. Some of this unease is the result of history – we do after all share roots with the Puritans, once defined by HL Mencken as people nagged by the fear that somewhere, someone else is having a good time. Together with the Quaker history of principled stand against worldly ways, we have inherited the notion that enjoyment is a frivolity, if not exactly reprehensible. Furthermore, the Quaker concern for social reform has made us only too aware that the world is full of injustice and violence, and that people routinely experience the kind of suffering that ought by rights to be unimaginable. Surely, against this background, it is obscene even to raise the possibility of enjoyment?

So I want to make it quite clear what I mean by enjoyment. It is not necessarily the same as happiness, pleasure, or having fun, although all these things are nice. The origins of the word give a better indication of its meaning in this context. Enjoyment comes from the old French word *enjoir*, a compound of *in* and *rejoice*. *To enjoy* is therefore to be in a state of rejoicing. I use 'enjoyment' by preference only because the word 'rejoicing' brings to mind images of Biblical characters with tambourines, and risks us taking the whole thing too solemnly again. (Religious people are quite capable of rejoicing solemnly.) The enjoyment I mean, then, is rejoicing in God's re-creational presence – however we perceive it – in every moment of our existence. It is not a frivolous adjunct to the serious business of life. To me it's what we were created for;

it's both bedrock and our goal.

This absolutely does not mean that people who are starving, bereaved, raped, abused, or having their homes shelled should enjoy the experience, or be able to rejoice within it. What I am suggesting is that the vision of *being in joy* is why we work for peace, justice or equality and respond to other people's suffering. Driven by the memory of creative love in our own lives, we want to restore others to a condition where they might enjoy it too.

And this, finally, is where the various threads about genetics, ethics, spirituality and play come together. I've suggested that far from being a trivial and irresponsible activity, playing is one of the most important religious activities that human beings perform. The Book of Proverbs personifies Wisdom as a separate being, playing in the presence of God, but this is poetry not theology. Wisdom does not exist independently of God, and in reality it is God who plays.

Playing provides a model for our attempts to make sense and use of the world's phenomena, including our efforts in genetic research and technology. Our own experience tells us that playing is most satisfactory when it is disciplined enough to acknowledge certain constraints: I drew particular attention to respect and relationship, both of which have implications for ethics. Instead of focusing on ethical behaviour as primarily a set of rules, it may be more accurate to see it as arising out of relationship and driven by the desire to sustain what connects us (to keep playing). Science, with genetics as my favourite example, is a particular method of exploring connections between human minds and the natural world – it may be a rather esoteric method, but at heart it's in the same business as playing in a sandpit, or religion. For some of us science has deeply spiritual aspects to do with the sense of *finding another presence* in the space we are exploring.

What makes the idea of play irreplaceable here for me is its connection to enjoyment. As I said in chapter 4, both playing music and the development of skills in child's play demand a daunting degree of self-discipline, bravery and sheer hard work. There has to be a reason why people do it, and in the case of child's play it can't be the promise of a future reward. A musician will slog through hours of practice for the carrot of better performance, but a toddler is unlikely to be similarly motivated. The reward is in the present; playing is enjoyable, across the whole spectrum from fun to passion to exultation.

There are lots of reasons why people want to do genetic research. One reason, the immediate reward for all the effort, is that we enjoy it – it can be fun, it can make us happy, and for some of us it's the best way we know of rejoicing. And I think even people for whom that isn't true can, as observers of science, share a little in our enjoyment.

Only a few of us are research scientists but without exception each of us is called to understand something of what science says about the world. Without that engagement we will never be able to ask or answer the ethical questions posed by our genetic skills. Everyone also has to make moral decisions, genetic or otherwise. Living a morally good life is often not easy, and again I think we do it because in a profound way we enjoy it; despite the fact that we get it so wrong, so often, at heart we come to life with the desire to live good lives. So whatever our different opinions about aspects of gene technology, we want very much to do right with it. I hope that what has come across in this book, and the lecture, is that this immense responsibility must be taken seriously, but not solemnly. If we could take on our moral work in gene technology with enjoyment rather than as our grim duty, there might be moments (fleeting, but enough to keep us going) when it really is rejoicing; when, without having manipulated a single gene, we become the kind of people we want to be.

GLOSSARY[1]

Allele: an allele is a variant form of a *gene*. Because each cell of an individual carries two copies of each gene, a person always has two alleles that may nevertheless be identical. 'Variant' does not mean 'abnormal', and the 'normal' or commonest form of a gene is also referred to as an allele. Different genes vary enormously in the number of different alleles they have, and in their distribution in the population.

Carrier: a carrier will have the *gene* associated with a particular condition but will not actually show it. Usually, this is because the condition is a recessive one: although the gene for the condition has been inherited from one parent, the 'normal' gene inherited from the other parent can compensate. In order to show the condition, a recessive gene must be inherited from both parents. Recessive genes are much more common than dominant ones, where inheriting only one copy of the gene is enough for a person to show the condition.

Cloning: the verb 'to clone' is used in several distinct ways. In *molecular biology*, cloning a *gene* means isolating a single gene from the others in the *genome*, and placing it in an artificial construction that allows many identical copies of the gene to be produced so that it can be studied or used. Reproductive cloning involves copying the genetic constitution of an adult organism and persuading the copy to develop into a new organism; this is technically not easy, and has only been achieved with a few species. Therapeutic cloning refers to the production of genetically identical tissues that can be used to study or, potentially, treat diseases.

---

1 Terms in **bold and italic** are defined elsewhere within the glossary.

DNA: deoxyribonucleic acid, the basic genetic material. The DNA molecule is a complex one, with a backbone of sugar and phosphate molecules to which are attached four different *nucleotides*. The order in which the nucleotides are strung along the DNA strand corresponds to the order in which the amino acids, that make up the *protein* the gene codes for, will be assembled.

Gene: the unit of inheritance. In *molecular biology*, it usually means a particular stretch of the *genome* that codes for a *protein* or part of a protein. This definition is not adequate to explain many of the complexities of gene structure and function. In addition, the DNA cannot make the protein by itself – various other molecules, including other proteins and molecules related to DNA, are required.

Gene therapy: attempts to treat a genetic disease by replacing or repairing an abnormal *gene* associated with the disease. A number of gene therapies are on trial, but the results to date have not been as convincing as hoped, and the extent to which gene therapy will ever be medically useful remains unclear. A distinction is drawn between somatic gene therapy, in which the cells of a grown child or adult are modified, and germ line gene therapy, in which the modification is made to the germ cells (i.e. egg or sperm) before fertilisation, or to the very early embryo. The effects of somatic therapy stop at the individual treated, whereas the effects of germ line therapy will be passed on to subsequent generations.

Genetic diagnosis: using the presence of a *gene* associated with a disease or disability, to diagnose the presence of the condition.

Genetic enhancement: the use of *genetic manipulation* to enhance, improve or extend an organism's capabilities. It is usually contrasted with *gene therapy*, which uses the same techniques to cure or treat a disease.

Genetic manipulation, genetic engineering, recombinant genetics: all these terms refer broadly to the various techniques for making changes to an organism's *genome*. Different specialists prefer one term to another; I have used them interchangeably throughout this book. I use the term gene technology for the large-scale implementation of these techniques within society.

Genetics: the study of heredity and biological variation. As a discipline, genetics is just over 100 years old.

Genetic testing: the process of analysing the *genome* of an individual to see if it contains gene variants (*alleles*) associated with particular traits. Genetic testing usually means testing for one or a few specific *genes*, in individuals known or suspected to be at risk. Genetic screening refers to the same process but applied to large numbers of people (e.g. if all babies are screened at birth), and increasingly to testing for a number of different genes rather than just one or two.

Genome: the total genetic content of a cell. This is split into smaller units called chromosomes, which usually come in pairs, one from each parent. Different species have different sized genomes and different numbers of chromosomes, and the number is not connected with evolutionary complexity: humans have 46 chromosomes in 23 pairs, scorpions have 4, bracken has 116.

Genotype: the genetic characteristics of an organism. This can mean the entire *genome*, but more usually refers to one or more *genes* of interest.

Homology, homologous: if a structure (such as an organ, or a *gene*) in one species is the same as/similar to a structure in another species, even if they do not perform the same function, they are considered homologous. Homologous structures have usually evolved from the same ancestral form.

Molecular biology: the study of the molecules involved in the structures and biological processes of living things. Much of molecular biology focuses on *DNA* and *proteins*. Similarly, molecular genetics is the study of the molecular processes of inheritance, and tends to pay most attention to the molecule DNA.

Monogenic: a characteristic associated with a single *gene*.

Nucleotide: a nucleotide, also known as a base, is the chemical subunit of which *DNA* and some related molecules are composed.

Phenotype: the physical characteristics of an organism. It can refer to the whole organism, or to specific features such as a disease. The phenotype depends on the associated *genotype* as well as on environmental and other factors. Moreover, different genotypes can produce identical phenotypes.

Polygenic: a characteristic associated with more than one *gene*.

Protein: proteins are large, complex chemicals made up of simpler units called amino acids. The order in which the amino acids are assembled is determined by the order of *nucleotides* in the *gene* coding for that protein.

Stem cell: during embryo development, cells become differentiated into specific types of tissue (e.g. muscle cells, nerve cells). Stem cells are cells that stay undifferentiated and (in theory) retain the ability to turn into many or all of the differentiated cell types. Because they retain this 'totipotency', they are important in *cloning*.

BIBLIOGRAPHY

Bains W. *Genetic Engineering for Almost Everybody*. Harmondsworth: Penguin, 1987

Camp CV. *Wise and Strange: An Interpretation of the Female Imagery in Proverbs in Light of Trickster Mythology*. In: Brenner A (ed), *A Feminist Companion to Wisdom Literature. The Feminist Companion to the Bible Vol 9*. Sheffield: Sheffield Academic Press, 1995, 131-156

Ellul J. *The Technological Society*. Trans. Wilkinson J. New York: Random House, 1964

Gilbert W. *A Vision of the Grail*. In: Kevles DJ and Hood L (eds), *The Code of Codes: Scientific and Social Issues in the Human Genome Project*. Cambridge: Harvard University Press, 1992, 83-97

Goodfield J. *Playing God: Genetic Engineering and the Manipulation of Life*. London: Hutchinson & Co, 1977

Gorski R. *New Scientist*, 28 September 1996

Hawking SW. *A Brief History of Time: From the Big Bang to Black Holes*. London: Transworld Publishers, 1990

Maitland S. *A Big-Enough God: Artful Theology*. London: Mowbray, 1995

Neumann-Held EM. *Let's Talk about Genes: the Process Molecular Gene Concept and its Context*. In: Oyama S, Griffiths PE, Gray RD (eds), *Cycles of Contingency*. Cambridge: MIT Press, 2001

Rehmann-Sutter C. *Contextual Bioethics. Perspektiven der Philosophie* 25, 1999: 315-338 (in English)

Scully JL. *Quaker approaches to to moral issues in genetics*. Lampeter: The Edwin Mellen Press, 2002

Thomas L. *The Medusa and the Snail: More Notes of a Biology Watcher*. Harmondsworth: Penguin, 1995

Tilby A. *Let There Be Light: Praying with Genesis*. London: Darton, Longman and Todd, 1989

Winnicott DW. *The Place Where We Live*. In: *Playing and Reality*. London: Routledge, 1991, 104-110

Science, spirituality and play

Not much has been written about the spiritual dimension of biological science. High on the list comes Annie Dillard, who writes in her own uncategorisable way about nature, investigation and the search for meaning. Her theology is often neither Quakerly nor comfortable but all her books are worth reading. *Pilgrim at Tinker Creek* is mostly natural history, *Teaching a Stone to Talk* includes the stunning essay *An Expedition to the Pole*. *Holy the Firm* is a short, unrelenting book about belief and pain; it contains some of Dillard's most difficult writing but repays the effort.

Barbara McClintock won the Nobel Prize in 1983 for decades of innovative work on maize genetics. Evelyn Fox Keller's biography, *A Feeling for the Organism: The Life and Work of Barbara McClintock* (WH Freeman & Co, 1984) is not ostensibly about either religion or belief but accurately describes the communion between scientist and the subject of investigation. Reading it will also tell you a lot about genetics, and the appalling isolation of a scientist whose ideas nobody else believes in. Mary Rose O'Reilly's *The Barn at the End of the World* (Milkweed, 2000) is subtitled *The Apprenticeship of a Quaker, Buddhist Shepherd*. It has nothing to do with genetics; but she writes about someone seeking, and finding, the 'deep peace of animal creation', without a trace of fluffiness. Adam Phillips' *Winnicott* (Harvard University Press, 1988) is a concise and very readable introduction to Donald Winnicott's life and work; some of Winnicott's own writing can be found in *Playing and Reality* (Routledge, 1991).

History

The best history of twentieth century genetics and molecular biology is Horace Freeland Judson's *The Eighth Day of Creation: Makers of the Revolution in Biology* (Cold Spring Harbor Laboratory Press, expanded edition published in 1996). It is based on interviews with the key players and uses much of their own words. Although of daunting length (700-odd pages in the paperback edition) it is gripping, accessible and beautifully written: parts of it move me to tears. James Watson's own account of the discovery of the structure of DNA, *The Double Helix* (Penguin, 1976), is usually recommended as a classic, but its youthful arrogance (forgiveable) and outrageous misogyny make it almost unreadable. If you do try it, some balance will be provided by Anne Sayre's biography *Rosalind Franklin and DNA* (Norton, 2000).

More than once in this book I have mentioned the human tendency to use new knowledge to reinforce our prejudices. For salutary reminders of how far this can go, read Stephen Jay Gould's *The Mismeasure of Man* (Penguin, 1987) and Daniel J Kevles' *In the Name of Eugenics: Genetics and the Uses of Human Heredity* (University of California Press, 1986).

Genetics and biotechnology

There are many books about genetics, genetic engineering and biotechnology, and new ones are coming out all the time. A clear, non-propagandising guide to the science and techniques of genetic manipulation can be found in Mark Walker and David McKay's *Unravelling Genes: A Layperson's Guide to Genetic Engineering* (Allen & Unwin, 2000). Steve Jones' *The Language of the Genes* (Flamingo, 2000) is also good. John Medina, in *The Genetic Inferno: Inside the Seven Deadly Sins* (Cambridge University Press, 2000), accessibly conveys the sheer complexity of the biological basis for various human behaviours.

In this book I have said little about the important subject of genetic manipulation in agriculture. Those interested should try *First Fruit: The Creation of the Flavr Savr™ Tomato and the Birth of Biotech Food* (McGraw-Hill, 2000), in which Belinda Martineau gives an insider's view of how the first genetically modified tomatoes were produced and what happens when science meets the world of business. Natalie Angier's *Natural Obsessions* (Virago, 2000) is a reporter's story of the early days of oncogene research (and not of 'the race to discover the cancer gene', despite the publisher's blurb); she's good on feelings and politics, and her labs sound like home to me.

Bioethics

For genetic ethics in general, try *The Code of Codes: Scientific and Social Issues in the Human Genome Project*, edited by Daniel J Kevles and Leroy Hood (Harvard University Press, 1992), and *The Troubled Helix: Social and Psychological Implications of the New Human Genetics*, edited by Theresa Marteau and Martin Richards (Cambridge University Press, 1996). Both of these contain a variety of essays, some more technical than others. *Improving Nature? The Science and Ethics of Genetic Engineering*, by Michael J Reiss and Roger Straughan (Cambridge University Press, 1996) provides a wide-ranging if superficial discussion. Those interested in further reading about bioethics and human rights should see the 1999 Oxford Amnesty Lectures published as *The Genetic Revolution and Human Rights* (Oxford University Press, 1999). *Unmasking Administrative Evil* by Guy B Adams and Danny L Balfour (Sage Publications, 1998), although not about genetics, provides potentially useful insights into how evil becomes manifest in the everyday practices of organisations. *Prenatal Testing and Disability Rights*, edited by Erik Parens and Adrienne Asch (Georgetown University Press, 2000), has a predominantly American flavour but contains an interesting range of voices from this debate.

The link between faith and bioethics is explored by the various contributors to *Notes From a Narrow Ridge: Religion and Bioethics*, edited by Dena S Davies and Laurie Zoloth (University Publishing Group, 1999). *Inventing Heaven? Quakers Confront the Challenges of Genetic Engineering*, edited by Amber Carroll and Chris Skidmore (Sowle Press, 1999), is already well known to British Friends. The work with British Friends that I undertook as Joseph Rowntree Quaker Fellow during 1995 and 1996 is detailed in *Quaker approaches to moral issues in genetics* (The Edwin Mellen Press, 2002).

TAKING IT FURTHER:
GETTING INVOLVED, GETTING INFORMED

A good first step would be to contact the Quaker Genetics and Ethics Network which is under the care of Bedfordshire General Meeting. Friends House (173 Euston Road, London NW1 2BJ, Tel. 020 7663 1000) will also be able to give up-to-date information about Quaker work in this area, especially on the work of the 'Earth: Our Creative Responsibility' group. The Quaker United Nations Office in Geneva (13 avenue du Mervelet, 1209 Geneva, Tel. 0041 22 748 4800, Fax 0041 22 748 4819) has done a lot of work in the areas of patenting and trade, and its publications can be found on its website (www.quno.ch). Woodbrooke Quaker Study Centre sometimes runs courses on related issues (1046 Bristol Road, Selly Oak, Birmingham B29 6LJ, Tel. 0121 472 5171, Fax 0121 472 5173 (www.woodbrooke.org.uk).

Reading *New Scientist* (www.newscientist.com) each week will keep you informed about what's going on in genetics (and other areas of science), and it doesn't shy away from critical appraisals of the social and political impacts.

The following organisations or bodies provide information and further contacts, sometimes with the possibility of active involvement. As there is no such thing as an unbiased source, discernment must be exercised in assessing the information given, and determining what else might be needed to complement it.

The Nuffield Council on Bioethics (28 Bedford Square, London WC1B 3JS, Tel. 020 7681 9619, Fax 020 7637 1712, www.nuffield-bioethics.org *[no hyphen]*) is an independent body established in 1991 to consider the ethical issues arising from developments in medicine and biology. The Council is funded jointly by the Nuffield Foundation, the Wellcome Trust and the Medical Research Council, and publishes a variety of reports, as does the Wellcome Trust itself (The Wellcome Building, 183 Euston Road, London NW1 2BE, Tel. 020 7611 8888, Fax 020 7611 8545, www.wellcome.ac.uk).

GeneWatch UK (The Mill House, Manchester Road, Tideswell, Buxton, Derbyshire SK17 8LN, Tel. 01298 871898, Fax 01298 872531, www.genewatch.org), The Genetics Forum (94 White Lion Street, London N1 9PF, Tel. 020 7837 9229, www.geneticsforum.org.uk) and Human Genetics Alert (Unit 112, Aberdeen House, 22-24 Highbury Grove, London N5 2EA, Tel. 020 7704 6100, Fax 020 7359 8423, www.hgalert.org) all provide a wide range of materials. The Gene Letter (c/o GeneSage, 589 Howard Street, Third Floor, San Francisco, CA 4105, USA, Tel. 001 415 371 9500, Fax 001 415 371 9501, www.geneletter.org) is similar but more US-based.

The home pages of the European Patent Office (www.european-patent-office.org) and the UK patent office (www.patent.gov.uk) give information about current policy and legislation on the patenting of genetically modified living organisms. Greenpeace (Canonbury Villas, London N1 2PN, Tel. 020 7865 8100, Fax 020 7865 8200, www.greenpeace.org) and Friends of the Earth (26-28 Underwood Street, London N1 7JQ, Tel. 020 7490 1555, Fax 020 7490 0881, www.foe.co.uk) both campaign against the 'patenting of life' and provide background information in support. Some of the transnational pharmaceutical and agrochemical companies will also provide information, from their websites or on request, to support *their* positions.

The Department of Health (Richmond House, 79 Whitehall, London SW1A 2NS, Tel. 020 7210 4850, minicom 020 7210 5025, www.doh.gov.uk) will link you to the Advisory Committee on Genetic Testing, the Gene Therapy Advisory Committee, the Genetics and Insurance Committee, and the Human Genetics Commission (www.hgc.gov.uk). These and other bodies often have public consultations on genetic and related issues (for example, the House of Lords Select Committee on stem cell research carried out a consultation exercise in autumn 2001); these are important opportunities to contribute your opinion.

STUDY QUESTIONS

Below are some questions for individual reflection or group discussion, loosely grouped by chapter. They are *suggestions* only, to be used as starting points for further exploration.

Quaker Resources for Learning has also produced the study pack *Playing God? Ethical and Theological Issues in Genetic Manipulation*, by Jackie Leach Scully, available from the Quaker Bookshop. This offers more ideas for working through problems of genetic ethics.

Chapter 1

1 What have your experiences of science been like – positive, negative, non-existent?
2 What words or images come to mind in connection with 'scientist'?
3 How do (or don't) you connect science and religion in your life?
4 Have you ever had any experience you would call 'spiritual' in connection with science or the natural world?

Chapter 2

1 When did you first hear about things like genetics, gene technology, genetic engineering, or cloning? Were your first impressions positive or negative ones?
2 What areas of life have been affected by gene technology? As an exercise in imagination, how do you see genetics affecting the world in a hundred years' time?
3 Does knowing that we have such a close genetic relationship with other animals and plants change your ideas about how we should behave towards them?

Chapter 3

1 Who do you think should have access to a person's genetic information?
2 Suppose we identify genes associated with various human characteristics, ranging from severe diseases to minor quirks of appearance, and can test for these prenatally, should there be limits to what can be tested for? If so, where should these limits be?

3 How would you feel if you were told that you were, in fact, a clone? What questions would you want to ask your parents?

4 What stands in the way of genetic manipulation being used to benefit the poorer world? What can be done about the obstacles?

Chapter 4

1 As we saw in this chapter, the phrase 'playing God' has a lot of different meanings. Do any of them make sense to you? What does this suggest to you about your understanding of play, and of God?

2 Read all of Proverbs chapter 8. Does the description of Sophia given here relate in any way to your own understanding of wisdom?

3 When, in your life, have you been at play?

Chapter 5

1 What do you think are our key moral responsibilities in gene technology?

2 What sources do you draw on for help in making moral evaluations and decisions?

3 Take the idea of finding a moral balance in a relationship of respect, and use it to explore one of the problematic areas in gene technology outlined in chapter 3 – cloning, for example, or prenatal genetic diagnosis, or patenting genetically modified organisms.

Chapter 6

1 How could we integrate molecular genetics and gene technology into a Quaker testimony to creation?

2 Can you identify marginalised or polarised groups involved in the genetic debate that might need help to communicate their views?

3 Have the ideas of genetics (or any other science) changed any of your ideas on topics like human nature, families, or the meaning of life?

4 In imagination, take a mindful walk through one of the mundane events mentioned in chapter 6 – visiting the doctor,

shopping for food, paying for medications, being ill or very young or very old. Where are the bioethical issues in these everyday experiences?

5 *Before* saying 'draft a Minute', how, in practice, can we bring Quaker corporate discernment to bear on genetic issues? Which Quaker processes and structures could we use, and how best would we use them?